THIS BOOK BELONGS TO...

_____

NAME...

_____

PHONE...

_____

Puzzle 1

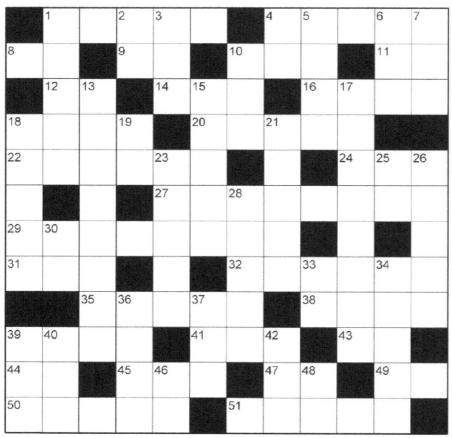

41. Highest mountain in Crete
43. Therefore
44. Otherwise
45. An age
47. Part of the verb to be
49. Perform
50. Skill
51. Aircraft field

DOWN
1. Plunges knife into
2. In the direction of
3. An explosive
4. Plural of I
5. Foot part
6. Zero
7. Abstract being
10. Prefix, three
13. Popular South African music
15. Greek theatre
17. Sensation
18. Examination of account books
19. Prefix meaning without
21. Dipper
23. Precipice
25. Hello there
26. Lyric poem
28. Assessed
30. Objective case of I
33. Similar to
34. Wear away
36. Smart - , show-off
37. Fish part
39. Chinese cooking implement
40. Sea eagle
42. Atmosphere
46. Satisfactory
48. Therefore

ACROSS
1. - voce, in a low tone
4. Pule
8. Neuter singular pronoun
9. Not off
10. Golf peg
11. Prefix meaning not
12. Part of the verb "to be"
14. Rocky peak
16. Long fish
18. Swedish pop-group of the '70s

20. Stupid people
22. Benefits derived from wealth
24. Definite article
27. Dignity of a lord
29. Having the form of an imago
31. Decade
32. Tormented
35. Faux pas
38. Father
39. Welt

Puzzle 2

ACROSS
1. Venezuelan river
4. Happen
8. Part of the verb "to be"
9. The ratio between circumference and diameter
10. Yoko -
11. Negative vote
12. Prefix meaning without
14. Soldiers
16. Auricular
18. Thailand
20. Nidi
22. Ingest
24. Television frequency
27. Auditor
29. Sufficiency
31. Also
32. Smells
35. Brown pigment
38. Wealthy
39. Mexican currency
41. Rotational speed
43. Therefore
44. Neuter singular pronoun
45. Hog
47. Similar to
49. Possessive form of me
50. Consumed
51. Pueblo Indian village

DOWN
1. Full speed
2. Toward the top
3. Edge
4. Not off
5. Diving bird
6. Prefix, one
7. Fabulous bird
10. Monad
13. Pearlescent
15. Abstract beings
17. Earthquake's tidal waves
18. Malay martial art
19. Objective case of I
21. Woodland deity
23. Take sounding
25. Masculine pronoun
26. Not stale
28. Steep slope
30. Perform
33. Otherwise
34. Pueblo Indian village
36. Sulk
37. Work unit
39. Pastry item
40. Greek letter
42. Raincoat
46. Prefix meaning not
48. Therefore

Puzzle 3

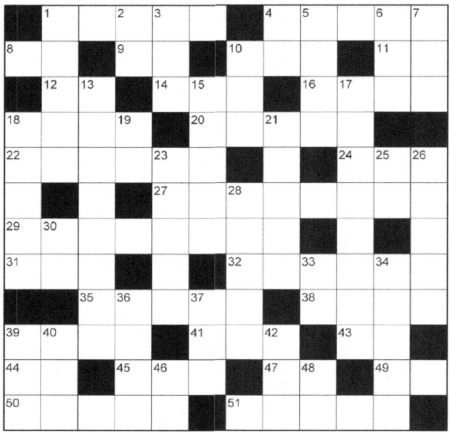

ACROSS
1. Amid
4. Cricket sundries
8. Bovine beast
9. Negative vote
10. Actor, - Gibson
11. The ratio between circumference and diameter
12. Part of the verb to be
14. An infusion
16. Egyptian goddess of fertility
18. Discharged a debt
20. Garment tuck
22. Arm joints
24. Exclamation of surprise
27. Unfriendlies
29. Folk instrument
31. America (Abbr)
32. Harm
35. First prime minister of India
38. Sea eagles
39. Obligation
41. Electrical unit
43. In the direction of
44. Similar to
45. Intention
47. Hello there
49. Possessive form of me
50. Smallest amount
51. Supple

DOWN
1. Situated on an axis
2. Not off
3. Negating word
4. Plural of I
5. Hip bones
6. Prefix, over
7. Sister
10. - de mer, seasickness
13. Hissing
15. English Derby city
17. Steadfast
18. Hidden
19. Perform
21. More
23. What one
25. Masculine pronoun
26. Australia vs England cricket trophy
28. Herb
30. Objective case of we
33. Objective case of I
34. Goblin
36. Nestling
37. Male sheep
39. Indian dish
40. Avail of
42. Greek letter
46. Neuter singular pronoun
48. Neuter singular pronoun

Puzzle 4

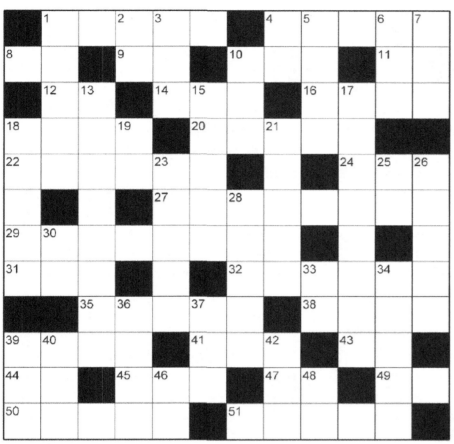

ACROSS
1. African river
4. Intertwine
8. Perform
9. Belonging to
10. Headache powder (Brand name)
11. Not off
12. Otherwise
14. Prefix, three
16. Church benches
18. Largest continent
20. Segment of the body of an arthropod
22. Copyist
24. - Maria, coffee liqueur
27. Excessive secretion of saliva
29. Hans Christian
31. Card game
32. Flights of steps
35. Fencing leap
38. Golf mounds
39. Surfboard fin
41. Mount - , N.W. Qld. mining town
43. Therefore
44. Masculine pronoun
45. Resinous deposit
47. Neuter singular pronoun
49. Providing
50. Relaxes
51. Slaver

DOWN
1. Lasso
2. Depart
3. Newt
4. Plural of I
5. Public exhibition
6. Promise
7. Abstract being
10. Ballpoint biro
13. Small domestic dove
15. Raves
17. Beings
18. Dismay
19. Part of the verb "to be"
21. Smiling
23. Fourth month
25. Part of the verb to be
26. Gather
28. Agreements
30. Negative vote
33. Near to
34. Lubricate again
36. Leer
37. Facial twitch
39. That woman
40. New Zealand parrot
42. Atmosphere
46. Similar to
48. In the direction of

Puzzle 5

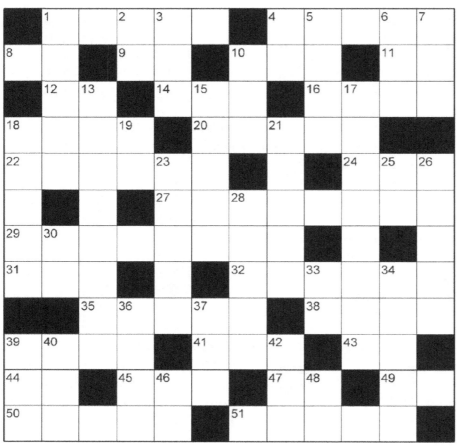

41. Large body of water
43. Negative vote
44. Similar to
45. Briefly immerse in water
47. Hello there
49. Providing
50. Leaven
51. Of a base

DOWN
1. Intoxicating
2. Objective case of we
3. Actor, - Chaney
4. Plural of I
5. Peruse
6. - Chi. Slow moving martial art form
7. Abstract being
10. Farewell
13. Raider
15. Cub leader
17. Will
18. Venezuelan river
19. Objective case of I
21. More pleasant
23. Book of the Bible
25. Near to
26. Wens
28. Gemstone
30. Not off
33. In the direction of
34. Mar
36. Mires
37. Extrasensory perception
39. Merry
40. Avail of
42. Exclamation of surprise
46. Neuter singular pronoun
48. Part of the verb to be

ACROSS
1. Single stem
4. Put pen to paper
8. To exist
9. Therefore
10. Hive insect
11. Prefix meaning without
12. Part of the verb "to be"
14. No
16. Rent-a-car company
18. First man
20. Japanese form of fencing

22. Nutlet
24. Resinous deposit
27. Liveliness
29. Food fibre
31. Finish
32. Person proficient in the arts
35. Ant
38. Expression used when accident happens
39. Hindu teacher

Puzzle 6

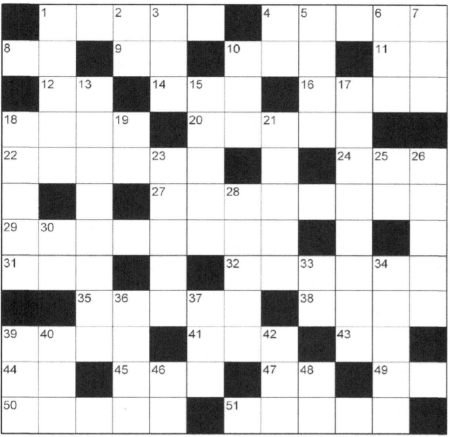

43. In the direction of
44. Part of the verb to be
45. Diving bird
47. Part of the verb "to be"
49. Therefore
50. Smears
51. Braid

DOWN
1. A watch
2. Negative vote
3. Black bird
4. Plural of I
5. Scion
6. - Guevara
7. Evil spell
10. Rotational speed
13. Elderly person
15. Harmonious sound
17. Infant's cradle
18. Abnormal body temperature
19. Objective case of I
21. Explode
23. Prefix, nose
25. The ratio between circumference and diameter
26. Stage whisper
28. Decease
30. Perform
33. Belonging to
34. Uneven
36. Reveal secret
37. Very good (1-2)
39. Concealed
40. America (Abbr)
42. Spoil
46. Objective case of we
48. Objective case of I

ACROSS
1. Mercenary
4. What one
8. Hello there
9. Not off
10. Female ruff
11. Masculine pronoun
12. Depart
14. Little devil
16. Mountain goat
18. Movie
20. Shadow
22. Church officials
24. Mineral spring
27. Excessive production of sweat
29. Imposing buildings
31. Gipsy lad
32. Made amends
35. Torpedo vessel (1-4)
38. Comrade
39. Throw
41. Electrical resistance

Puzzle 7

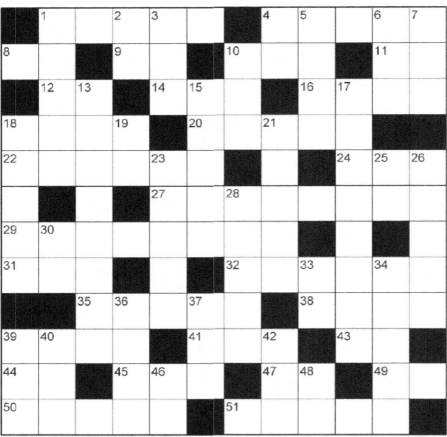

41. Open
43. Part of the verb "to be"
44. Not off
45. Musical instrument
47. In the direction of
49. Bovine beast
50. Leans
51. Lord's home

DOWN
1. Seashore
2. The ratio between circumference and diameter
3. Bad
4. Masculine pronoun
5. To the sheltered side
6. Fire remains
7. Negating word
10. Public transport
13. Receiving a salary
15. Unit of light
17. Region in S Italy
18. Room
19. To exist
21. Sound
23. Republic in W Africa
25. Prefix meaning without
26. Short stalk
28. Razor strap
30. Toward the top
33. Plural of I
34. Defense covering
36. Indian peasant
37. Fox
39. Iota
40. Prefix, one
42. Greek letter
46. Objective case of we
48. Not off

ACROSS
1. Two-legged support
4. Brother of Abraham
8. Objective case of I
9. Providing
10. Unit of loudness
11. Therefore
12. Similar to
14. Influenza
16. Authentic
18. Strike breaker
20. Pale green mosslike lichen
22. Mucus
24. - Vegas, US gambling city
27. Hesitating
29. Seedless raisins
31. Prefix, over
32. Do up parcel again
35. Muse of poetry
38. Ireland
39. Wife of Punch

Puzzle 8

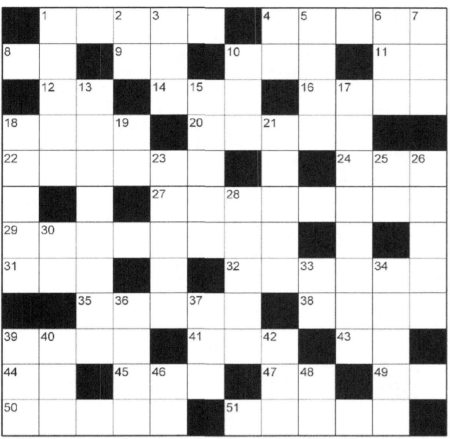

ACROSS
1. Ravine
4. Silly
8. Not off
9. Negative vote
10. Fireplace ledge
11. To exist
12. Providing
14. Influenza
16. Radar screen element
18. Frizzy hair style
20. Surround
22. Cause hearing loss
24. Outfit
27. Infinite time
29. Casual coatlike garment
31. Australian bird
32. Sweeping implements
35. Bailiff
38. Photograph of bones (1-3)
39. Greek goddess of the earth
41. Room within a harem
43. Possessive form of me
44. Similar to
45. Tier
47. Depart
49. Prefix meaning without
50. Slink
51. Navigation aid

DOWN
1. - and fork
2. Not off
3. Money (Slang)
4. Perform
5. Swedish pop-group of the '70s
6. Law enforcement agency
7. Yes
10. Drone
13. Break
15. Slow
17. Lyre shaped
18. Sun-dried brick
19. Belonging to
21. Wood-eating insect
23. Weird
25. Neuter singular pronoun
26. Wanderer
28. Waned
30. Part of the verb "to be"
33. Bovine beast
34. Yucatan indian
36. Nobleman
37. Promise
39. Vapour
40. Question
42. In the past
46. Satisfactory
48. Otherwise

Puzzle 9

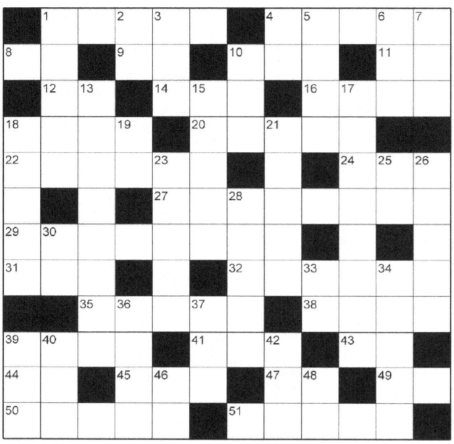

ACROSS
1. Intoxicating
4. Tramps
8. Negative vote
9. Objective case of I
10. Beak
11. The ratio between circumference and diameter
12. Plural of I
14. An age
16. Crude minerals
18. As well as
20. Master of ceremonies
22. Trouble
24. That woman
27. Russian mystic
29. Stirs
31. Fish eggs
32. Tidier
35. Nymph presiding over rivers
38. Expression
39. Assess
41. Mount - , N.W. Qld. mining town
43. Perform
44. Bovine beast
45. Musical instrument
47. In the direction of
49. Therefore
50. Income
51. Monetary unit of Lesotho

DOWN
1. Bawls
2. Part of the verb "to be"
3. Scottish river
4. Masculine pronoun
5. Hautboy
6. Open
7. Sister
10. Vietnam
13. Hungry, greedy
15. Took examination again
17. Said again
18. Fragrant oil
19. Otherwise
21. Thicket
23. Inhabitant of Iraq
25. Hello there
26. Huge
28. Dispatches
30. Depart
33. Near to
34. Uneven
36. Great age
37. Assist
39. Gipsy lad
40. Chop
42. Dined
46. Objective case of we
48. Not off

Puzzle 10

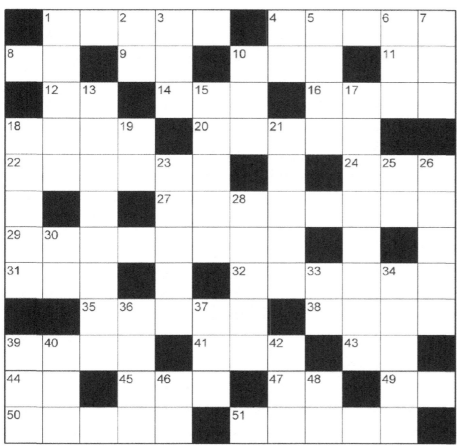

44. Bovine beast
45. Printer's measures
47. In the direction of
49. Therefore
50. Overgrown with wild plants
51. Move to music

DOWN
1. Lifeless
2. Prefix meaning not
3. Very good (1-2)
4. Hello there
5. Ancient Greek coin
6. Fish eggs
7. Arid
10. Handwoven Scandinavian rug
13. Recounts
15. Ant
17. Halted through lack of wind
18. Dials
19. The ratio between circumference and diameter
21. Unrefined
23. European mountains
25. Near to
26. Intervening
28. Renee -, Australian rock singer
30. Objective case of I
33. Belonging to
34. Uneven
36. Require
37. Raises
39. Promise
40. Chop
42. Greek letter
46. Possessive form of me
48. Not off

ACROSS
1. Assumed name
4. Accumulate
8. Part of the verb "to be"
9. Negative vote
10. Chest bone
11. Otherwise
12. Not off
14. Unlocking implement
16. Heed
18. Bind securely (Nautical)
20. Twinned crystal
22. Skylighted lobby
24. Eccentric wheel
27. Control
29. Issued
31. Become firm
32. Naval clerks
35. Follow
38. Comrade
39. Urn
41. Prefix, before
43. Perform

Puzzle 11

43. Affirmative vote
44. Joint in the hind leg of a horse
46. Every
50. Lavatory (Colloq)
51. 12th month of the Jewish calendar
52. Bound
53. Bawl
54. Advise
55. Oceans

DOWN
1. Hairpiece
2. Acknowledgement of debt
3. Two
4. Collection of samples
5. Mops
6. Swine
7. I have
8. Wise old man
9. Rich soil
10. Australian super-model
11. Roman dates
19. U-turn (Colloq)
21. Prefix meaning not
22. Female horse
23. Maturing agent
24. Scheme
25. Sweet potato
27. Cove
28. Indian queen
29. Woe is me
30. Stop
32. Nave
33. Small bits of food
35. Fuss
36. To and -
37. Objective case of I
38. Leg joint
39. Fine powder
40. 8th month of the Jewish calendar
41. Flock of quail
42. Driving shower
45. Bullfight call
47. Falsehood
48. New Zealand parrot
49. Commercials

ACROSS
1. Senses
5. Reel
9. Garland
12. U.S. State
13. Marry
14. Aged
15. Pacific island U.S. naval base
16. Matures
17. Beer
18. Hotels
20. Occasions
22. Acers
25. Over there
26. Awry
27. Metal rod
28. Cheer
31. Back
32. Overact
33. Monetary unit of Western Samoa
34. Sea eagle
35. Purchase
36. Last
37. Unruly crowd
38. Person proficient in the arts
39. Himalayan country
42. Scorning person

Puzzle 12

44. Bulb flower
46. Wyatt -
50. Beak
51. Noose
52. Ostrich-like bird
53. Bitter vetch
54. Ornamental brooch
55. Faucets

DOWN
1. Sick
2. New Zealand bird
3. In the past
4. Crazy
5. Pond scum
6. 8th month of the Jewish calendar
7. Missus
8. Dissepiment
9. Ancient town in N Africa
10. Capital of Yemen
11. Mast
19. Abstract being
21. Masculine pronoun
22. Type of automatic gear selector (1-3)
23. Indian queen
24. Towards the centre
25. Hold up
27. Pastry item
28. Skin
29. The villain in Othello
30. Prepare patient for operation
32. Legal right
33. Hazelnut
35. Art of dueling
36. Cracker biscuit
37. The ratio between circumference and diameter
38. Pictograph
39. Sensible
40. Maturing agent
41. Debutantes
42. Political combine
45. Acknowledgement of debt
47. Exclamation of surprise
48. Corded fabric
49. Dance step

ACROSS
1. Officiating priest of a mosque
5. Intentions
9. Annihilate
12. Booth
13. Harp-like instrument
14. Fuss
15. South-east Asian nation
16. Pant
17. Actor, - Gibson
18. Perceive sound
20. Baron
22. Three in one
25. Regret

26. Explosive sounds
27. Small long-haired dog
28. Fruit seed
31. Rectangular pier
32. Crane boom
33. Terror
34. - de Janeiro
35. Owing
36. Blockade
37. Purulence
38. Fast horse gait
39. Cleaning lady
42. Jelly-like mass
43. Mature

Puzzle 13

ACROSS
1. Beehive
5. Type of automatic gear selector (1-3)
9. Concealed
12. Prefix, air
13. Potpourri
14. Fuss
15. Unique thing
16. Dry riverbed
17. Beer
18. You
20. Beer
22. Fuse pottery or glass
25. Seine
26. Tetrads
27. Musical instrument
28. Missus
31. Questions
32. Nave
33. Flesh
34. Cereal
35. Metal rod
36. A dance
37. Cat's sound
38. Prison guard
39. Chief Anglo-Saxon god

42. First class (1-3)
43. To endure
44. Boss on a shield
46. Noisy
50. A fool
51. Man
52. Narrow country road
53. Golf peg
54. Reared
55. Migrant farm worker

DOWN
1. Cracker biscuit
2. Knowledge
3. Before
4. Doorkeepers
5. Drying cloth
6. Blue-gray
7. Assist
8. Vexed
9. Dutch name of The Hague
10. Lazy
11. Performer
19. Owns
21. Near to
22. Distant
23. Inquisitive
24. Use atomic bom on (Colloq)
25. Gist
27. Of us
28. Merge
29. Garden tool
30. Leading player
32. Utterance of hesitation
33. Sour cherry
35. Deaden
36. Kitchen utensil
37. Objective case of I
38. Courted
39. Desire
40. Off-Broadway theater award
41. Unit of force
42. Capable
45. Spoil
47. Large tree
48. Prefix, one
49. Scottish river

Puzzle 14

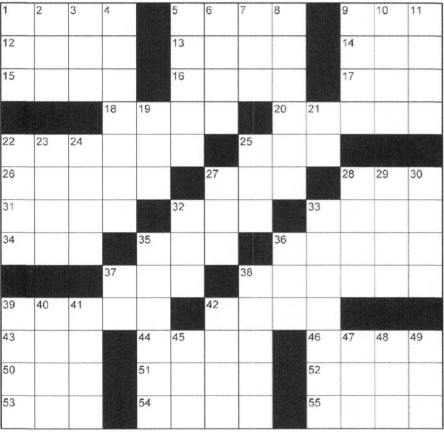

44. Through
46. Is indebted
50. Monad
51. Sled
52. Scorpion-like N.Z. insect
53. Monetary unit of Japan
54. Personalities
55. A join

DOWN
1. My, French (Plural)
2. Choose
3. An infusion
4. Book of the New Testament
5. Hives
6. Without
7. Finish
8. Take weapons from
9. Member of the women's army auxiliary corps
10. Jason's ship
11. Printer's mark, keep
19. Bitter vetch
21. Therefore
22. Sacks
23. Egg-shaped
24. Lethargic
25. A craze
27. Jack in cribbage
28. Praise
29. Fencing sword
30. Former Soviet Union
32. Price on application (Abbr)
33. Woes
35. Condition
36. Actress, - Farrow
37. The ratio between circumference and diameter
38. Depressed spirits
39. Things in favour of something
40. Narrow country road
41. Capital of Yemen
42. Jason's ship
45. Embrace
47. Tiny
48. Greek letter
49. Uncle -, USA personified

ACROSS
1. Nocturnal insect
5. Second-hand
9. Once existed
12. Fencing sword
13. Indian queen
14. Talent
15. Pierce with knife
16. Finishes
17. Mature
18. Clarets
20. English race course
22. Short jacket
25. To and -

26. Confesses
27. Vietnam
28. Monetary unit of Romania
31. Silences
32. Seed vessel
33. Undermines
34. Wily
35. Watch pocket
36. Pouts
37. Legume
38. Bird-watcher
39. Braid
42. Having wings
43. Radiation unit

Puzzle 15

42. Smear
43. Fruit seed
44. Welsh emblem
46. Motor car
50. Beer
51. Australian super-model
52. Hit with hand
53. Decade
54. Primordial giant in Norse myth
55. Suffix, diminutive

DOWN
1. Goad for driving cattle
2. Yoko -
3. Indicate assent
4. Italian dumplings
5. Persian fairies
6. Ancient Greek coin
7. Seed vessel
8. Hay fever reaction
9. Tubular pasta in short pieces
10. Smart - , show-off
11. Legumes
19. Not at home
21. The ratio between circumference and diameter
22. Overwhelmed
23. Nip
24. Fever
25. Raises
27. Diving bird
28. Natural fibre
29. Small island
30. Particoloured
32. Flying mammal
33. Crowning molding of a pedestal
35. U.S. sharpshooter
36. Greek letter
37. Depart
38. Creator
39. Gaiter
40. Mound
41. Candid
42. Delicatessen
45. Shady tree
47. Last month
48. Make lace
49. Open

ACROSS
1. Percussion instrument
5. Bursts
9. Annihilate
12. Soon
13. Black
14. Island (France)
15. Extinct bird
16. Travelled on
17. An infusion
18. Curl
20. Heroic tales
22. Counting frame
25. Israeli submachine gun

26. Any living being
27. Primate
28. Small drink
31. Sewing case
32. Public transport
33. Spanish words of agreement (2.2)
34. Scottish river
35. Large tree
36. Thin silk net used in dressmaking
37. Gun (Slang)
38. Striking
39. Ghost

Puzzle 16

43. First woman
44. Use atomic bom on (Colloq)
46. Ancient Greek coin
50. Conger
51. Son of Isaac and Rebekah
52. Molten rock
53. Attempt
54. Assess
55. Minor oath

DOWN
1. Information
2. Top card
3. Which person
4. Bishop of Rome
5. Make amends
6. Wind instrument
7. Japanese sash
8. Fittingly
9. Whirlpool
10. Pout
11. Pip
19. Last month
21. Belonging to
22. Codlike fish
23. To the sheltered side
24. Nee
25. Work unit
27. Flu (Colloq)
28. Ward off
29. Hindu music
30. Scent
32. Fairy
33. Access hole
35. A messenger
36. Facial twitch
37. To exist
38. Waiting line
39. English court
40. Finished
41. Depend
42. Card game
45. America (Abbr)
47. Sack
48. Eggs
49. Boy

ACROSS
1. Gape
5. Small particle
9. Printer's measures
12. Reverberate
13. Pipe
14. Female deer
15. Lighting gas
16. Off-Broadway theater award
17. Owing
18. Food fish
20. Flirted
22. Dexterous
25. Fairy

26. High up
27. Crooked
28. To and -
31. Cut made by a saw
32. Thick mist
33. Honey liquor
34. Even (poet.)
35. Tatter
36. Ballroom dance
37. Purchase
38. Monetary unit of Albania
39. Actress, Sophia -
42. Similar

Puzzle 17

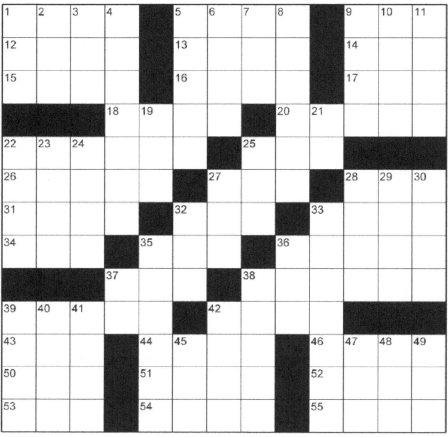

ACROSS
1. Fetid
5. Car registration (Colloq)
9. Large body of water
12. Ursa
13. Taverns
14. Beldam
15. Identical
16. Solicit
17. I have
18. Once again
20. Inamorato
22. Card suit
25. Irk
26. Went wrong
27. Otic organ
28. Extrasensory perception
31. Student at mixed school
32. Avid admirer
33. French cheese
34. Two
35. Prefix, whale
36. Stoppers
37. Cove
38. Eager
39. Confused mixture of sounds
42. Catch
43. Wood sorrel
44. Eager
46. Jealousy
50. Allow
51. 8th month of the Jewish calendar
52. New Guinea currency unit
53. Before
54. Agile
55. Stalk

DOWN
1. Observation
2. Meadow
3. Braggart (Colloq) (1.2)
4. Greatly feared
5. Rituals
6. Enough
7. Wildebeest
8. Stableman
9. Switchblade
10. Roof overhang
11. Maturing agent
19. - Kelly
21. Bovine beast
22. Cult
23. Front of ship
24. Region
25. Forefront
27. Consume
28. Sea eagle
29. Portent
30. Nuisance
32. Doomed
33. Monetary controls
35. Seaport in N France
36. Brassiere
37. To exist
38. Irate
39. Tree trunk
40. The maple
41. Restrain
42. Fly high
45. Swindle
47. Negating word
48. Victory sign
49. Sweet potato

Puzzle 18

39. Waned
42. Ku Klux -
43. Female ruff
44. Sewing case
46. Ostentatious
50. Goad for driving cattle
51. Travel on
52. Skin opening
53. Poem
54. Elide
55. Struck

DOWN
1. Soak flax
2. Bullfight call
3. High-pitched
4. Fits new back parts to shoes
5. Clever
6. Monetary unit of Nigeria
7. Dined
8. Bank cashier
9. Tiller
10. Double curve
11. Hired thug
19. Prefix, one
21. Objective case of we
22. Cab
23. Intentions
24. Rich soil
25. Blend
27. Fairy queen
28. Spanish words of
   agreement (2.2)
29. Soon
30. Sharp pain
32. Gave food to
33. Abducts
35. High waterproof boots
36. Bleat
37. To exist
38. Aviator
39. Therefore
40. Necklace component
41. English monk
42. African antelope
45. Sesame plant
47. Gipsy lad
48. Prefix, three
49. To date

ACROSS
1. Lion's call
5. Card game
9. Pig
12. Australian super-model
13. Dust speck
14. The self
15. 9th letter of the Hebrew
   alphabet
16. Cain's victim
17. Zodiac sign
18. Wallaroo
20. Unit of light
22. Skill

25. My, French (Plural)
26. Garlic-flavored mayonnaise
27. Russian community
28. Vital tree fluid
31. Christmas
32. Machine for sending
   documents
33. Basic currency of Papua New
   Guinea
34. Doctrine
35. Spider's structure
36. American buffalo
37. Evil
38. Losing colour

Puzzle 19

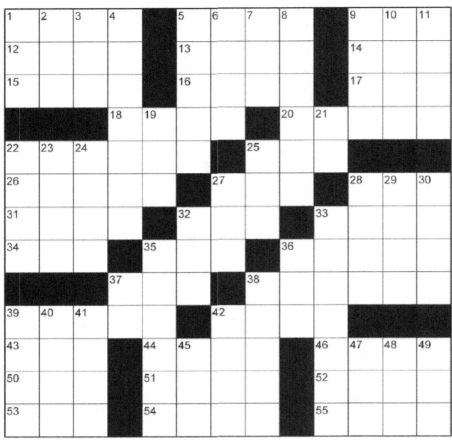

42. Leading player
43. Not at home
44. Resembling ink
46. Employs
50. Island (France)
51. Put to sea
52. Hindu garment
53. Vietnam
54. Stimulate
55. Trumpet

DOWN
1. Bleat
2. Raises
3. Small drink
4. Moslem woman's veil
5. Greek letter
6. 20th letter of the Hebrew alphabet
7. Question
8. Adult mayfly
9. Scorning person
10. Wool package
11. Prophet
19. - and outs, intricacies
21. Neuter singular pronoun
22. Capable
23. Den
24. Arm bone
25. U-turn (Colloq)
27. Expression of contempt
28. Jot
29. Small remnant
30. Relax
32. Decay
33. Papyrus
35. Uncouth
36. Actress, - Farrow
37. To exist
38. Manner
39. Piece of money
40. Hawaiian dance
41. A particular
42. Jump
45. No
47. Cracker biscuit
48. Go wrong
49. Transgress

ACROSS
1. Active
5. Toward the mouth
9. Ethnic telecaster
12. Capital of Western Samoa
13. Rocky tableland
14. Not
15. Egyptian serpents
16. Portable ice-box
17. Bullfight call
18. Lofty
20. Slender filament
22. Woman graduate
25. Last month

26. Red variety of spinel
27. Turkish governor
28. Carp-like fish
31. Nexus
32. Sunbeam
33. Aboriginal rite
34. An age
35. Exclamation of wonder
36. Speechless people
37. Flying mammal
38. Green fodder preserved in store
39. Tribe ruler

Puzzle 20

42. U.S. State
43. Expression of disgust
44. Donated
46. Small children
50. Golf peg
51. Fencing sword
52. Wrongfully assist
53. Before
54. Hire
55. Linelike

DOWN
1. Evil
2. Female ruff
3. Land measure
4. Large marsupials
5. Marsh plants
6. Appends
7. Negative
8. Ringings of bells at death
9. Pitcher
10. Give food to
11. Decades
19. Island (France)
21. Part of the verb "to be"
22. Temple
23. Hautboy
24. Father
25. Otic organ
27. Common eucalypt
28. Maori image
29. Related
30. Untidy state
32. Machine for sending documents
33. Polar
35. Jerk rapidly
36. - Chi. Slow moving martial art form
37. Negative vote
38. Bedding item
39. Silent
40. Maturing agent
41. Clarified butter
42. Baking chamber
45. Primate
47. Japanese sash
48. Decade
49. Pig enclosure

ACROSS
1. Excellent
5. Tier
9. Newt
12. Prefix, air
13. Paradise
14. Tiny
15. Consider
16. Brink
17. Even (poet.)
18. Offers a price
20. Fats
22. Prickly pears
25. Shady tree

26. Wane
27. Vapour
28. Scottish cap
31. Expression used when accident happens
32. Animal pelt
33. Spear point
34. Large body of water
35. Fruit conserve
36. Maori images
37. Water sprite
38. Junipers
39. Gog and - (Agents of Satan)

Puzzle 21

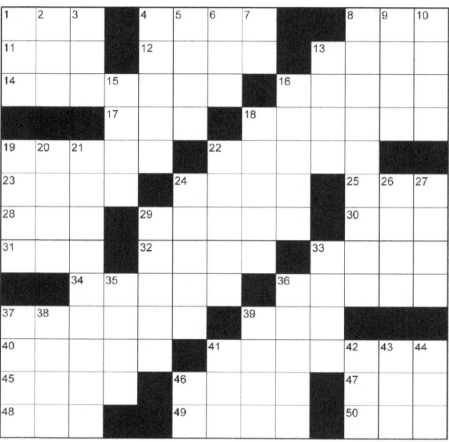

ACROSS
1. Influenza
4. Grain store
8. Mount - , N.W. Qld. mining town
11. Sicken
12. Ku Klux -
13. Songbird
14. Particulars
16. Unit for measuring gold
17. Commercials
18. Title for a woman
19. Pomes
22. Quick
23. Existence
24. Prefix, air
25. Braggart (Colloq) (1.2)
28. Food scrap
29. Light meal
30. Atomic mass unit
31. Golf peg
32. Verne's submariner
33. Inflammation (Suffix)
34. Vexes
36. Type of turnip
37. Free from confinement
39. Snow runner
40. Draws close to
41. Ryot
45. Vehicles
46. Spoken
47. Fish eggs
48. Open
49. Furl
50. Greek letter

DOWN
1. A craze
2. Falsehood
3. Last month
4. Slides
5. Woes
6. - Vegas, US gambling city
7. Not off
8. Illuminate
9. A join
10. Poker stake
13. Dry riverbed
15. River in central Switzerland
16. Pillow stuffing
18. - Polo
19. Plan
20. Ireland
21. Convalescent care
22. Bores out
24. Anoint
26. Among
27. Ponder
29. Drags logs
33. Certainly
35. Paddles
36. Scandinavian poet
37. Remarkable
38. Lowest high tide
39. Marine mammal
41. In favour of
42. Land measure
43. Negating word
44. An infusion
46. Belonging to

Puzzle 22

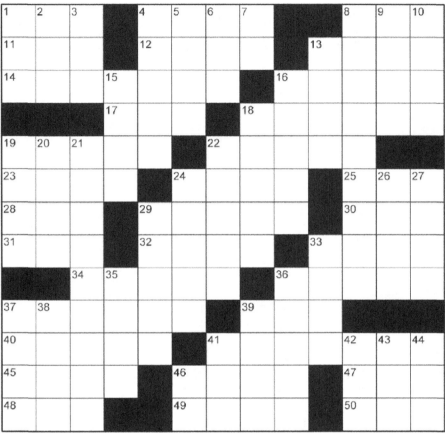

39. Male offspring
40. Jumps
41. True blue (5-2)
45. Scandinavian
46. Ruse
47. Money (Slang)
48. Before
49. Long fish
50. Television frequency

DOWN
1. Comforter or quilt
2. Some
3. Russian community
4. Norwegian dramatist
5. Opera solo
6. Vapour
7. Not off
8. Residence of monks
9. Prude
10. Abode
13. 9th letter of the Hebrew alphabet
15. Migrant farm worker
16. Person foolishly fond of another
18. Outmoded
19. Illegally fixes result
20. Hip bones
21. City view
22. Yucatan indians
24. Soil
26. Sewing case
27. Curse
29. Pennants
33. Humid
35. Scandinavian
36. Regions
37. Australian super-model
38. Close to
39. Window ledge
41. Expire
42. Acknowledgement of debt
43. Scale note
44. If and only if
46. Plural of I

ACROSS
1. Overact
4. The villain in Othello
8. Miles per hour
11. Black bird
12. Grain husk
13. Bull
14. Heartburn
16. Jeans fabric
17. New Zealand parrot
18. Senility
19. Powder from castor-oil plant
22. Mathematics

23. Tennis star, - Natase
24. Fence opening
25. Spread out for drying
28. British, a fool
29. Pilot
30. Greek letter
31. Utter
32. Heavy metal
33. Thrum
34. Thick slices
36. 7th letter of the Hebrew alphabet
37. Coop up

Puzzle 23

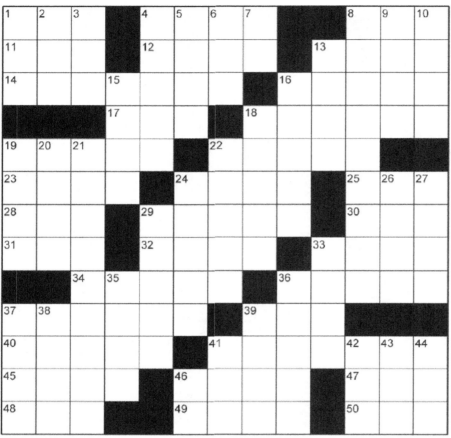

40. Think
41. Fanlike posterior of crayfish
45. Flesh
46. Cripple
47. Be indebted
48. Conger
49. Shrill bark
50. Prefix, the earth

DOWN
1. Merry
2. Monad
3. Sicken
4. Dress which flares from top (1-4)
5. Accustomed
6. Ovum
7. Perform
8. Liver disease
9. To the sheltered side
10. Scottish hills
13. Steals from
15. Whip
16. Praises
18. Irish county
19. In addition to
20. Part played
21. Occurring every eight years
22. Stoppers
24. Tremble
26. Applies friction to
27. Gaelic
29. To drink deeply
33. Wool fibre
35. Isn't
36. Dress with care
37. A few
38. Fencing sword
39. Appendage
41. - kwon do (Korean martial art)
42. Thick mist
43. Reverential fear
44. Prefix, new
46. Possessive form of me

ACROSS
1. Tibetan gazelle
4. Overwhelmed
8. Taxi
11. Black bird
12. Business emblem
13. Anger
14. Shouting
16. Actress, Sophia -
17. Social insect
18. Cavalry sword
19. Ordinary writing
22. To redden

23. Scottish lake
24. One pound sterling
25. Crude mineral
28. Last month
29. Stoppers
30. Prefix, over
31. Witness
32. The villain in Othello
33. Person in authority
34. Police informers
36. Body of deputised hunters
37. Infirm through old age
39. Prefix, three

Puzzle 24

39. Exclamation of surprise
40. Zodiac sign
41. Dramatize
45. Stand
46. Of urine
47. Twosome
48. Exclamation of disgust
49. Cry-baby
50. Nocturnal precipitation

DOWN
1. Metal bar
2. Biblical high priest
3. Once common, now banned, insecticide
4. Indian term of respect
5. Reward
6. W.A. river
7. Depart
8. Enjoin
9. Relax
10. Group of two
13. Siamese
15. American Indian
16. Mediterranean vessel
18. Capital of Tunisia
19. Demonstration
20. Member of the women's army auxiliary corps
21. Set up
22. Tilts
24. Dull people
26. American university
27. Prayer ending
29. Intestinal obstruction
33. Nautical call
35. Double curve
36. Shanty
37. Alter
38. Opera solo
39. Potpourri
41. In favour of
42. Sum
43. Prompt
44. Haul
46. Objective case of we

ACROSS
1. Colour
4. Polluted atmosphere
8. Prefix, foot
11. Aged
12. Prefix, air
13. Salver
14. Got rid of
16. Bantu language
17. Free
18. Tormented
19. Nerd
22. Having the form of a cube

23. Relax
24. Curse
25. Handwoven Scandinavian rug
28. Floor rug
29. Grecian architectural style
30. Braggart (Colloq) (1.2)
31. Wood sorrel
32. Many
33. Capable
34. South Africans
36. Gloss
37. Bowlegged

Puzzle 25

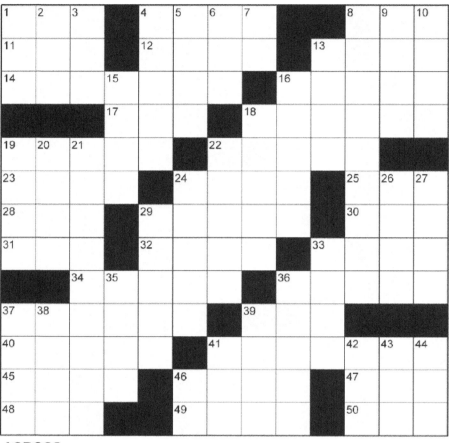

ACROSS
1. Definite article
4. Dutch name of The Hague
8. Skilled
11. Of us
12. Reverberate
13. Verne's submariner
14. Daisy-like flower
16. Sprinter
17. Carp-like fish
18. Solidus
19. Villeins
22. Icy
23. Willing
24. Sensible
25. The self
28. Land measure
29. Oscillated
30. Doze
31. Scottish hill
32. Assistant
33. Gael
34. British soldier
36. Scots
37. Ancient Mycenaean

ceramic piece
39. 3 Thickness
40. Manila hemp plant
41. Ryot
45. Not any
46. Property title
47. Veer
48. Social insect
49. Leer
50. Greek letter

DOWN
1. To clothe
2. Colour
3. Go wrong
4. Obeys
5. Land measure
6. Exclamation of surprise
7. Depart
8. Moral decay
9. Prayer ending
10. Low-quality diamond
13. Follower of Hitler
15. Punch
16. Fit new supports on chair
18. The sesame plant
19. Thick slice
20. Ireland
21. Pointing inward
22. Garish
24. Moves in water
26. Jail
27. Chooses
29. South Pacific Islands
33. States
35. At one time
36. Valley
37. Japanese syllabic script
38. Black
39. Skin
41. Wooden pin
42. Affirmative vote
43. Singer, - "King" Cole
44. Two
46. Perform

Puzzle 26

ACROSS
1. Two
4. Prayer
8. Talk
11. Exclamation of surprise
12. Dregs
13. Prison room
14. Latin
16. Stop
17. Scottish expression
18. Farm implement
19. One-celled protozoa
22. Cover with dew
23. Pierce with horn
24. Clutched
25. Coxa
28. Revised form of Esperanto
29. Commotion
30. Greek letter
31. Negative
32. Therefore
33. Skin
34. Lookers
36. Ointments
37. Solitary
39. Island of Denmark
40. Confesses
41. A sailor
45. Chief god of ancient Greece
46. Rice wine
47. Monad
48. Abstract being
49. Poems
50. Tibetan gazelle

DOWN
1. - Chi. Slow moving martial art form
2. Buddhist temple
3. Exclamation of surprise
4. Fold
5. Wife of Jacob
6. Even (poet.)
7. Similar to
8. Cogwheel
9. As well as
10. Gusted
13. Wax
15. Ear part
16. Container for storing items
18. A greeting
19. Against
20. Style
21. Arousing sexually
22. South African mountains
24. Haste
26. A particular
27. Friends
29. Feet parts
33. Glass panel
35. Evergreen trees
36. Units of computer memory
37. Loll
38. Baking chamber
39. Bogus
41. Insane
42. Large tree remnant
43. Yoko -
44. An infusion
46. Therefore

Puzzle 27

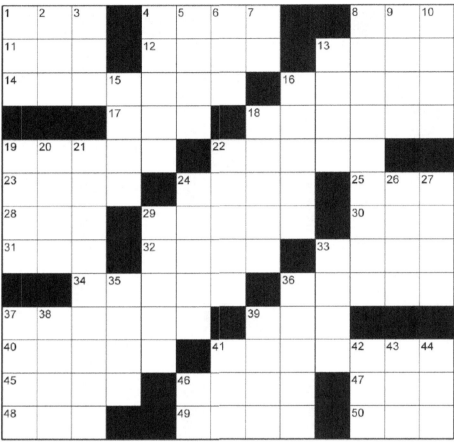

ACROSS

1. Hold up
4. Car registration (Colloq)
8. Law enforcement agency
11. Monad
12. 8th month of the Jewish calendar
13. Pond
14. Ogre
16. Garlic-flavored mayonnaise
17. Spread out for drying
18. Steal cattle
19. Wind instruments
22. Wild
23. Islamic chieftain
24. Scene of first miracle
25. Sphere
28. Government broadcaster
29. Swiss song
30. Exclamation of surprise
31. Also
32. Once again
33. Consumer
34. Efts
36. Wash
37. Locality
39. Prefix, not
40. Gather
41. Recompenses
45. Grotto
46. American coin
47. Diving bird
48. Before
49. Scent
50. Tibetan gazelle

DOWN

1. Gipsy lad
2. Yoko -
3. Scottish hill
4. Rituals
5. Looked over
6. Needlefish
7. Otherwise
8. Free to travel about
9. Cotton seed vessel
10. Tennis star, - Natase
13. Italian city
15. Leading player
16. Pertaining to the ear
18. Modernise
19. Nipple
20. Boss on a shield
21. Concave on both sides
22. Loses colour
24. Fable
26. Ostrich-like bird
27. Nee
29. Sailing vessels
33. Arm bone
35. Relax
36. Shrink from
37. Openwork fabric
38. - Khayyam
39. Verne's submariner
41. Free
42. Tatter
43. Twosome
44. Jamaican popular music
46. Perform

Puzzle 28

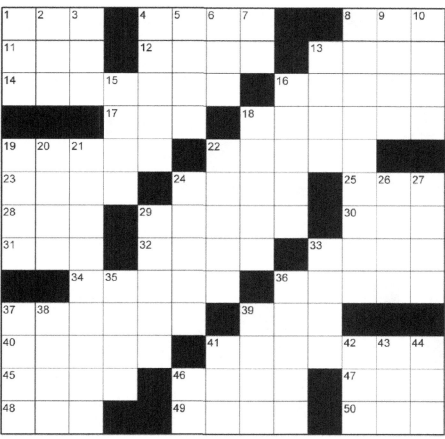

ACROSS
1. Soldiers
4. Sacred Egyptian bird
8. Gymnasium
11. Dined
12. Something not to be done (2-2)
13. Blue-gray
14. Works hard
16. Decants
17. Brassiere
18. Re-marries
19. French queen, - Antoinette
22. In a fit manner
23. Wrongfully assist
24. Grotto
25. - Kelly
28. Government broadcaster
29. Bread maker
30. French, water
31. Actress, - West
32. Ireland
33. Surreptitious, attention getting sound
34. African antelope
36. Saunter
37. Scriptural
39. Expire
40. Pay for grazing
41. Leaping
45. Floating ice
46. Neck hair
47. Bleat
48. Marsh
49. Ova
50. To date

DOWN
1. - de mer, seasickness
2. Greek letter
3. Beak
4. Habituate
5. Aboriginal rite
6. - and outs, intricacies
7. Therefore
8. Stickiness
9. Length measure
10. Untidy state
13. Large dish
15. Funeral notice
16. An apostle
18. Split
19. Madam
20. Swedish pop-group of the '70s
21. Critical revision of a text
22. Hundu mendicant
24. Song
26. Relax
27. Obligation
29. Procreate
33. Bard
35. Church recess
36. Long distances
37. Fishing hook
38. Leer
39. Damn
41. Droop
42. To endure
43. Not
44. Make lace
46. Objective case of I

Puzzle 29

ACROSS
1. Play on words
4. New Zealand parrot
8. Conger
11. Yoko -
12. Sacred Egyptian bird
13. Yucatan indian
14. Lacking
16. Adored
17. Superlative suffix
18. Salad vegetable
19. Electric discharge
22. Roof overhangs
23. Baton
24. Visage
25. - and don'ts
28. Part of a circle
29. Pond scum
30. Cheer
31. Expression of contempt
32. Former coin of Spain
33. London district
34. A parent
36. Ruined
37. Proclaim
39. Rummy game
40. White vestment
41. Prickled
45. Bird of prey
46. Valuable metal
47. Dined
48. Before
49. Chances
50. Crow call

DOWN
1. Captive soldier
2. Prefix, one
3. Negating word
4. Refreshment stand
5. Adjoin
6. Pack
7. Similar to
8. Listen clandestinely
9. Looker
10. Refined woman
13. Breakwater
15. Flock of cattle
16. Flood embankment
18. Chocolate nut
19. Mop
20. Prefix, beyond
21. Hermit
22. Tidal wave
24. Capable of flowing
26. Island of Hawaii
27. Fired a gun
29. Muddle
33. Carolled
35. Openwork fabric
36. Varieties
37. Codlike fish
38. Islamic chieftain
39. Coat with gold
41. Fox
42. Resinous deposit
43. Greek letter
44. Nocturnal precipitation
46. Depart

Puzzle 30

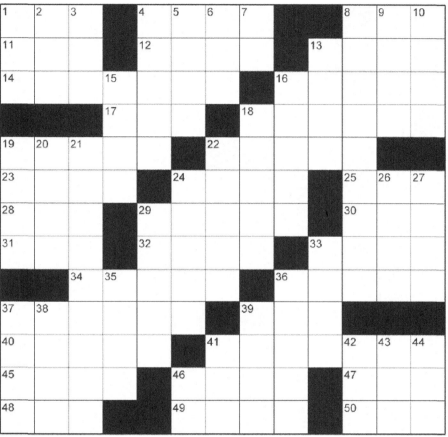

41. Related by birth
45. Rocky tableland
46. Wool package
47. Braggart (Colloq) (1.2)
48. Bitter vetch
49. Pitcher
50. Monetary unit of Romania

DOWN
1. A swelling
2. Mature
3. 10th letter of the Hebrew alphabet
4. Lace placemat
5. Cain's victim
6. Distress signal
7. Masculine pronoun
8. School canteens
9. Every
10. Short take-off and landing aircraft
13. Line roof
15. Information
16. Hood-shaped anatomical part
18. Public swimming pool
19. Staunch
20. 6th month of the Jewish calendar
21. Tautness
22. Turned towards
24. Gem surface
26. Unwrap
27. Time of prosperity
29. Did not
33. On top of
35. Soft lambskin leather
36. Keen
37. Identical
38. River in central Europe
39. Foot part
41. Crow call
42. Sicken
43. - kwon do (Korean martial art)
44. Australian bird
46. To exist

ACROSS
1. Method
4. Sprint
8. It is
11. The self
12. Hautboy
13. Sect
14. Donkeys
16. Small lizard
17. Everything
18. Deepest lake in the world
19. Containing fat
22. Cataracts
23. Notion
24. Destiny
25. Nave
28. Fled
29. Russian country house
30. Yoko -
31. Missus
32. Frozen confections
33. Upswept hairdo
34. Finished
36. English Derby city
37. Voiced
39. Cracker biscuit
40. Skilled

Puzzle 31

37. Emphatic form of it
40. Weary
41. Disorderly flight
42. Complete
46. Heroic
47. Heavy metal
48. In favour of
49. Third son of Adam
50. Harp-like instrument
51. Sister

DOWN
1. Limb
2. Eggs
3. Lycanthrope
4. Mimicry
5. Moslem demon
6. Play division
7. Temerity
8. Drags logs
9. Silence
10. Lazy
11. Slew
16. Shopping centre
20. Notion
21. An enthusiast
22. Hautboy
23. Celts and Gaels
25. Overthrow
26. Pictures taken at close range (5-3)
27. Listen attentively
28. Days before
30. Flunk
34. Blackbird
35. Bring
36. Electrical rectifier
37. Angers
38. Drink to excess
39. Matching outfit
40. Russian emperor
43. Turkish governor
44. Prefix, three
45. Greek goddess of the dawn

ACROSS
1. Base
4. Slightly open
8. Switchblade
12. First woman
13. Size of type
14. Naked
15. Apparel
17. Small island
18. Merit
19. Upper
21. Having prominent jowls
23. Finishes

24. Ancient Greek coin
25. Endure
26. - Guevara
29. Mountain pass
30. Cavity
31. Lavatory (Colloq)
32. State of drowsy contentment
33. Inspires dread
34. Extra
35. Fish appendages
36. Writing tables

Puzzle 32

ACROSS
1. 3 Thickness
4. Flaky mineral
8. Surreptitious, attention getting sound
12. Handwoven Scandinavian rug
13. Object of worship
14. Prefix, eight
15. Weirdness
17. Diving bird
18. Fate
19. Regardless
21. Things owing
23. Pace
24. Opera solo
25. Just
26. Pastry item
29. An evergreen
30. Group of six
31. Hallucinogenic drug
32. Spread out for drying
33. Shakespeare's river
34. Phoned
35. Submachine gun
36. Infested with vermin
37. Fisherman
40. The villain in Othello
41. Jaguarundi
42. Urgency
46. Smell foul
47. Bargain event
48. Anger
49. Gaelic
50. Obey
51. Worthless dog

DOWN
1. Prefix, before
2. Soap ingredient
3. Convict
4. Son of Zeus
5. As previously given
6. Long-leaved lettuce
7. German shepherd
8. Coral builder
9. Barge
10. Portico
11. Swank
16. Jot
20. Dweeb
21. Foolish
22. A Great Lake
23. Of English descent
25. Febrile
26. Free from sensual desire
27. Is not
28. Nervous
30. Detest
34. Hindu music
35. Serpent
36. Assessed
37. Withered
38. Looker
39. Angers
40. Small island
43. Not
44. French vineyard
45. Your (Colloq)

Puzzle 33

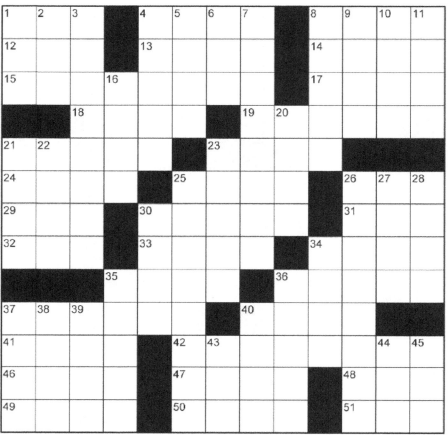

37. Although
40. Skilfully
41. 8th month of the Jewish calendar
42. Not practicable
46. Small drink of liquor
47. Empty
48. Clumsy person
49. Long fish
50. Gaelic
51. To date

DOWN
1. Humorous person
2. Crude mineral
3. Weirdness
4. Weighty
5. Jaguarundi
6. A charge
7. Quivers
8. Simpleton
9. Egg
10. Singer, - Lynn
11. Soon
16. Atmosphere
20. Great age
21. Inspires dread
22. Verne's submariner
23. Oilcan
25. Having the power to heal
26. Hired hoodlum
27. Responsibility
28. Food regimen
30. Mongolian desert
34. Festival
35. Expressions
36. Live
37. Assistant
38. Harp-like instrument
39. False god
40. Rent-a-car company
43. And not
44. New Guinea seaport
45. Newt

ACROSS
1. Alas
4. Heave
8. Exploding star
12. Land measure
13. Looker
14. Baking chamber
15. Sterile
17. Former coin of Spain
18. Jot
19. Insane person
21. Bother
23. Heed

24. Unwanted plant
25. Grain store
26. A person
29. Printer's measures
30. Physician
31. Prefix, one
32. Distress signal
33. Single items
34. Paste
35. Type of automatic gear selector (1-3)
36. City in central Belgium

Puzzle 34

40. Prefix, large
41. Having wings
42. Triangular
46. Riding strap
47. Upswept hairdo
48. - Guevara
49. Refuse
50. Struck
51. Consume

DOWN
1. Deity
2. To endure
3. Most dangerous
4. Refine my melting
5. Cab
6. Black bird
7. Baseball pitched at the batter's head
8. Lake in the Sierra Nevada
9. Woe is me
10. Tree trunk
11. Hardens
16. Tall and thin
20. Earthen pot
21. Ran from
22. Prefix, air
23. Greek writer of fables
25. Debris
26. Annulment
27. Assistant
28. Swing to the side
30. Russian emperor
34. Car registration (Colloq)
35. Person employed by a carnival
36. Procreated
37. Reddish brown chalcedony
38. To the sheltered side
39. Willingly
40. Skirt coming to just below knee
43. Rotational speed
44. Exclamation of surprise
45. Allow

ACROSS
1. Needlefish
4. Pierce with knife
8. Labels
12. Japanese sash
13. Neck hair
14. Agave
15. Impairment in reading ability
17. Stop
18. Wife of Shiva
19. Lassoes
21. Lacking brightness
23. Capable

24. Welsh emblem
25. Trade agreement
26. Vessel or duct
29. Bitter vetch
30. Unit of magnetic induction
31. Lubricant
32. Speck
33. Short take-off and landing aircraft
34. Travel on
35. Freshwater fish
36. Cover with dew
37. Hunting expedition

Puzzle 35

ACROSS
1. Slack
4. Mimicked
8. Floor rugs
12. Monad
13. Withered
14. Off-Broadway theater award
15. Toward the wind
17. Arm bone
18. Spoken
19. Small isles
21. Oriental nation
23. Gael
24. Having aches
25. Ember
26. Greek goddess of the dawn
29. Which person
30. Photograph
31. A couple
32. Monetary unit of Japan
33. Tarn
34. Property title
35. Employer
36. Infectious blood disease
37. Australian airline
40. Submachine gun
41. Viper's tooth
42. Ideal quality
46. Capital of Western Samoa
47. Cultivate
48. Pedal digit
49. Ecstatic
50. Shout
51. Over there

DOWN
1. Base
2. Black bird
3. Greek historian
4. Dam extending across the Nile
5. Ring of bells
6. Go wrong
7. Consecrate
8. Shed feathers
9. Capable
10. Hue
11. Oceans
16. Cart
20. Performance by one
21. Chins
22. Pain
23. Cry-babies
25. Moral purity
26. Infinite time
27. One who is indebted
28. Alkali
30. Plan
34. Grudge fight
35. Gave birth to (Bible)
36. Booth
37. Distant
38. Soft lambskin leather
39. Pare
40. Vend
43. Expire
44. Also
45. Japanese currency

Puzzle 36

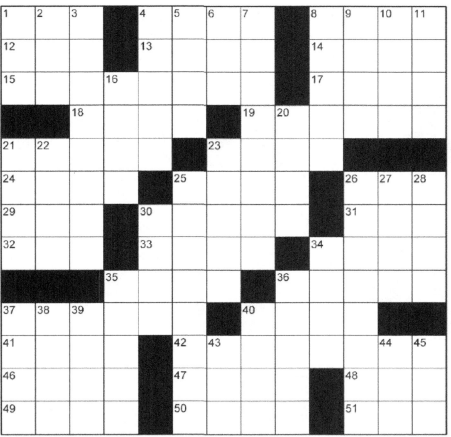

36. Verses
37. Spinning
40. Parched
41. University head
42. Science of winemaking
46. Stupefy
47. Taverns
48. Tibetan gazelle
49. Toboggan
50. June 6, 1944
51. Scale note

DOWN
1. Missus
2. U-turn (Colloq)
3. Insanity
4. Images
5. Breakwater
6. Black bird
7. Person who repairs machinery
8. Crocodiles (Colloq)
9. Egg part
10. Drudge
11. Whirlpool
16. French cheese
20. Non-scientific studies
21. Shank
22. First class (1-3)
23. Levis
25. Leaflike
26. Andirons
27. First man
28. Staffs
30. Russian emperor
34. Work hard
35. Languished
36. Resembling prose
37. Appends
38. Welt
39. Obscurity
40. Indian currency
43. Finish
44. Sticky stuff
45. Exclamation of disgust

ACROSS
1. Mire
4. Officiating priest of a mosque
8. Type of inflorescence
12. Female ruff
13. Ice-cream holder
14. Crucifix
15. Serving as a symbol
17. Fetid
18. Sea eagle
19. Jagged
21. Dog genus

23. Jolts
24. Routine
25. Confined
26. Distant
29. Prefix, one
30. Siamese citizens
31. Revised form of Esperanto
32. Large body of water
33. Synchronize
34. Type of jazz
35. Friends

Puzzle 37

40. Tree trunk
41. Iridescent gem
42. Hermitic
46. Levee
47. Ostrich-like bird
48. Pedal digit
49. Beats by tennis service
50. Male offspring
51. Not at home

DOWN
1. Piece
2. Avail of
3. SE Asian country
4. Took by force
5. Woe is me
6. Soak flax
7. Levels of command
8. Greek goddesses of the seasons
9. Woe is me
10. Dossier
11. Having pedal digits
16. Days before
20. Applies friction to
21. Impudent child
22. First class (1-3)
23. Knife
25. Breaks into many pieces
26. Forced high notes
27. Double curve
28. Spawning area of salmon
30. Ku Klux -
34. Indonesian resort island
35. Pulls
36. Unconsciousnesses
37. Alkali
38. Heroic
39. Fine
40. "Has - ". Person who once was
43. 17th letter of the Greek alphabet
44. Acknowledgement of debt
45. Prefix, whale

ACROSS
1. Hobo
4. Uncommon
8. Handle of a knife
12. Mount - , N.W. Qld. mining town
13. Smart - , show-off
14. Potpourri
15. Mind reader
17. Death rattle
18. Birds
19. Rubbed out
21. Howled as a hound
23. Sky colour
24. Antarctic explorer
25. Untidy person
26. In favour of
29. Black bird
30. Persian lords
31. Mature
32. An infusion
33. Youths
34. Lost blood
35. Detest
36. Looked over previous to robbing
37. Sitting

Puzzle 38

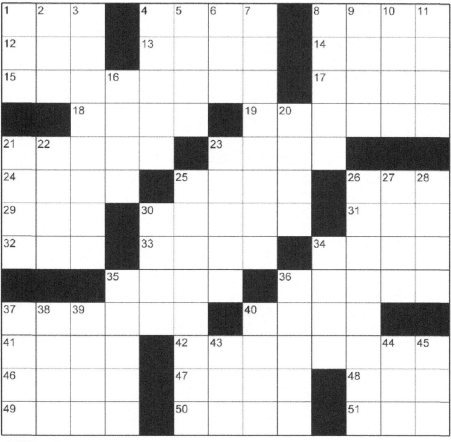

ACROSS
1. Take to court
4. Islamic chieftain
8. Summit of a small hill
12. Mature
13. Sensible
14. Indian queen
15. Phraseology
17. Military detachment
18. Officiating priest of a mosque
19. An African antelope
21. New York resort island
23. As soon as possible
24. Submachine gun
25. Ostentatious
26. Cheer
29. My, French (Plural)
30. The Earth
31. First woman
32. Commercials
33. Donkey call
34. Row
35. Temple
36. Perfume with incense

37. District adjacent to a city
40. Group of two
41. Toward the mouth
42. Frozen confection (3-5)
46. Once existed
47. Ember
48. Biblical high priest
49. Without
50. Foot part
51. King

DOWN
1. Vital tree fluid
2. Expression of disgust
3. Weirdness
4. Short story
5. Cripple
6. Tavern
7. Office where specific details are kept
8. German manufacturer of armaments
9. Grandmother
10. Indigo
11. Middle Eastern bread
16. Prayer ending
20. Yucatan indian
21. Unconsciousness
22. Was indebted
23. Rich tapestry
25. Vigorous exercises
26. Antlered animals
27. Birds
28. In this place
30. Type of automatic gear selector (1-3)
34. Rip
35. Naked pictures
36. Recurrent pattern
37. Female pigs
38. Fertiliser
39. Farm shed
40. Trade agreement
43. Dove's call
44. Beer
45. Blend

Puzzle 39

ACROSS
1. Relation
4. Fine dry soil
8. Greek god of love
12. Biblical high priest
13. Son of Isaac and Rebekah
14. See
15. Foul
17. Nautical, below
18. Greek goddess of strife
19. Church officials
21. Notice of an intended marriage
23. Paste
24. Matures
25. Cormorant
26. Uncle -, USA personified
29. Sister
30. Dutch shoes
31. Optic organ
32. Abstract being
33. Stand
34. Struck
35. Ecstatic
36. Fishing net
37. Be miserly
40. Ku Klux -
41. Chill
42. Levels of command
46. Wheel shaft
47. Thoroughfare
48. Monetary unit of Albania
49. Hairless
50. Male offspring
51. Greek letter

DOWN
1. State of drowsy contentment
2. Island (France)
3. Pleasantness
4. Delicatessens
5. Employs
6. Japanese word of respect
7. Instruction
8. Avoid
9. Anger
10. Scent
11. Stitches
16. Vases
20. Projecting pieces
21. Bottom
22. Against
23. Spook
25. Winter footwear
26. American indian
27. 16th letter of the Hebrew alphabet
28. Measure out
30. Pack fully
34. Marine mammal
35. Angered
36. Toboggans
37. Strike breaker
38. Hip
39. Trundle
40. Persian lord
43. Dove's call
44. Seine
45. Jamaican popular music

Puzzle 40

ACROSS

1. Church bench
4. Heroin
8. Splendour
12. Monad
13. Cultivate
14. Cain's victim
15. Suitable
17. Something not to be done (2-2)
18. Accolade
19. Gulp down
21. South American weapons
23. Employs
24. Parched
25. Epic poetry
26. Battle
29. Top card
30. Considers
31. Beer
32. - Vegas, US gambling city
33. Sea eagle
34. Ceases living
35. Network
36. Woman
37. Grave
40. Angers
41. Persian lord
42. Compelled
46. Isn't
47. Gentle
48. Paddle
49. Sorrows
50. Eye inflammation
51. Attempt

DOWN

1. Price on application (Abbr)
2. Finish
3. Magazines such as The Australasian Post
4. Breeding horses
5. Goodbye
6. High-pitched
7. Merry
8. Sharp pains
9. Ancient Greek coin
10. List of dishes
11. Plan
16. Quadrangle
20. Scottish headland
21. False god
22. Killer whale
23. Turn upside down (2-3)
25. Weirdness
26. Wooden panel
27. Smart - , show-off
28. 20th letter of the Hebrew alphabet
30. Suffix, skin
34. Antlered beast
35. Men
36. Put pen to paper
37. Skagen
38. U.S. State
39. Narrow country road
40. Full of unresolved questions
43. Negating word
44. Otic organ
45. Arid

Puzzle 41

41. Salt of iodic acid
43. Burn with water
46. Person foolishly fond of another
47. Having parts deleted for moral purposes
49. Assistant
52. Fuss
53. Indonesian resort island
54. Smear
55. Scottish hill
56. Heroic
57. Beak

DOWN
1. Dog variety
2. Anger
3. Republic in E Africa
4. Women collectively
5. Rime
6. Fitting
7. Russian emperors
8. Peruse
9. Male deer
10. Greek goddess of strife
12. Jump
17. Brawny
19. Doctor
21. Belly
22. Female sheep
23. Irregular
26. Room within a harem
28. Selenographer
29. Got down from mount
30. Hawaiian goose
32. Negates
37. Drunkard
40. Sun-dried brick
42. Deceased
43. Strike breaker
44. Yield
45. Soon
46. Delicatessen
48. Knock with knuckles
50. Owing
51. Wane

ACROSS
1. Mine
4. Eh?
8. That woman
11. European mountain range
13. Expression used when accident happens
14. Automobile
15. Hereditary factor
16. Beautiful, seductive spy (4.4)
18. Seaport in W Yugoslavia
20. Small animals

21. Instrument used in combat
23. Donkey
24. Grain beard
25. Hew
27. Ku Klux -
31. Hitler's autobiography, "-Kampf"
33. Poem
34. Christmas
35. Son of Isaac and Rebekah
36. Paddles
38. A fool
39. Boy

Puzzle 42

ACROSS
1. Fairy
4. Prophet
8. Taxi
11. Ostrich-like bird
13. Funeral fire
14. Japanese sash
15. Sweet potatoes
16. Proclaimed
18. Suffix, diminutives
20. Freshwater ducks
21. Smaller
23. An infusion

24. Biblical high priest
25. Ireland
27. Scottish church
31. Quote
33. Is able to
34. Primordial giant in Norse myth
35. Obey
36. Church recess
38. Pressure symbol
39. Conger
41. Masters of ceremonies

43. Fronded plants
46. Beginning
47. Petty quarrel
49. Hoarfrost
52. Total
53. Helps
54. Personalities
55. Faucet
56. Throw
57. Choose

DOWN
1. Cook in oil
2. Exclamation of surprise
3. Inhabitant of Yemen
4. Globular
5. Sight organs
6. Go wrong
7. Consumed again
8. Musical ending
9. Cain's victim
10. Offers a price
12. Italian wine province
17. Full of holes
19. Golf peg
21. Technical college (Colloq)
22. Tennis star, - Natase
23. Tautness
26. Knock with knuckles
28. Contagious skin infection
29. Stand
30. Malay dagger
32. Dropsy
37. Printer's measures
40. Convocation of witches
42. Wax
43. Surreptitious, attention getting sound
44. Blue shade
45. Nodule
46. One's parents (Colloq)
48. Prefix, life
50. Swab
51. Superlative suffix

Puzzle 43

ACROSS
1. Transgress
4. A bloke
8. Nautical, rear
11. Having wings
13. First class (1-3)
14. Prefix, life
15. Father
16. Capable of being cut
18. Timber tree
20. Brightly coloured lizard
21. Black magic
23. Biblical high priest
24. Donkey
25. Black
27. Gaiter
31. Hip bones
33. Consume
34. Cab
35. Be defeated
36. Region
38. Female ruff
39. Information
41. Emulates
43. Asian nation
46. Leather strip
47. Greek dish
49. Thaw
52. Sum
53. Sewing case
54. Egyptian deity
55. My, French (Plural)
56. University head
57. Secret agent

DOWN
1. Vital tree fluid
2. Island (France)
3. State of drowsiness
4. Seed of the cacao tree
5. Time unit
6. Social insect
7. Flower part
8. Swedish pop-group of the '70s
9. Movie
10. New Guinea currency unit
12. Marsh plant
17. Pay for grazing
19. Female deer
21. Let sink
22. Capital of Norway
23. Amuse
26. Paddle
28. Ramparts
29. Jump in figure skating
30. Binds
32. Sponsorship
37. Atmosphere
40. Relaxed
42. Adventuress
43. Officiating priest of a mosque
44. Knob
45. Clothes
46. Predatory sea bird
48. Dined
50. Fold
51. Your

Puzzle 44

ACROSS
1. Annihilate
4. Root vegetable
8. Apex
11. A Great Lake
13. Prefix, eight
14. Eggs
15. English college
16. Frightful
18. Composition for nine
20. Top card of suit
21. Room for action
23. Witness
24. Island (France)
25. Portable ice-box
27. At the apex
31. Rage
33. Norse goddess
34. The Pentateuch
35. Otherwise
36. Leer
38. Raincoat
39. Allow
41. Battle fleet
43. Burn with water
46. Belief involving sorcery
47. Capital of Finland
49. Metal holder for a coffee cup
52. Room within a harem
53. Skullcap
54. Pitcher
55. Each
56. Three (Cards)
57. Unlocking implement

DOWN
1. Letter Z
2. Talent
3. Early colonists
4. Golfing stroke resulting in one over par (5.4)
5. Authentic
6. Greek letter
7. Flavour
8. Beancurd
9. Egg
10. Insect feeler
12. Enough
17. Behave towards
19. Not
21. Existence
22. 12th month of the Jewish calendar
23. Divide into syllables
26. Beer barrel
28. Small axe
29. Toward the mouth
30. Large almost tailless rodent
32. Shouts
37. Before
40. Decree
42. Labyrinth
43. Store
44. Yield
45. Having wings
46. Migrant farm worker
48. And not
50. Female ruff
51. Cook in oil

Puzzle 45

Empire
46. Musical instrument
47. Book published annually
49. Opera solo
52. Attempt
53. Lazy
54. Skin
55. Greek goddess of the dawn
56. Rip
57. Yoko -

DOWN
1. Purulence
2. Monad
3. Vigorous resisters
4. Pellet of hail
5. Merely
6. Lubricant
7. Talent
8. Off-Broadway theater award
9. Diving bird
10. Norseman
12. Decorate (Xmas tree)
17. Armistice
19. New Guinea seaport
21. American grey wolf
22. Hawaiian feast
23. Janitor
26. Not
28. Musical composition
29. Small island
30. Marsh plant
32. An anaesthetic
37. Lair
40. Planet's path
42. Slightly open
43. Unit of computer memory
44. Prefix, air
45. Inlets
46. South American weapon
48. Poem
50. Tavern
51. Fuss

ACROSS
1. Seed vessel
4. Foot of a horse
8. Aged
11. Military detachment
13. Indigo
14. Large snake
15. Prophet
16. Inference
18. Full of hills
20. Greek goddess of peace
21. South American beasts
23. French vineyard

24. Of us
25. Sicilian volcano
27. Coconut husk fibre
31. Past tense of bid
33. Paddle
34. Gaelic
35. Evict
36. Require
38. Beer
39. Gardening tool
41. Having nipples
43. Founder of the Mogul

Puzzle 46

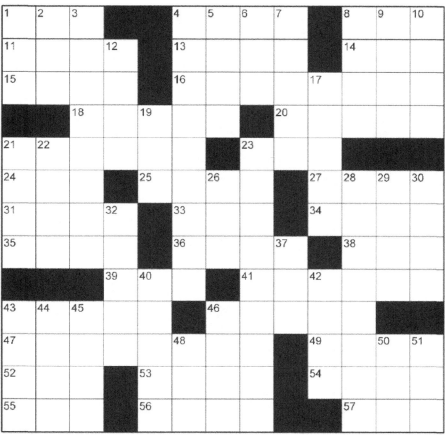

ACROSS
1. 10th letter of the Hebrew alphabet
4. Dictator
8. Curtsy
11. Hautboy
13. Second-hand
14. Chop
15. Former Soviet Union
16. Relied (on)
18. More secure
20. Bearings
21. German emperor
23. Kitchen utensil
24. Open
25. Yelps
27. Glimpse
31. Rent
33. Not
34. Portico
35. Girl
36. Shank
38. Social insect
39. Scale note
41. Charm
43. Asian country

46. The earth
47. Exclusion
49. Fat
52. Fruit conserve
53. Gooey (Colloq)
54. A Great Lake
55. Anger
56. Appear
57. Put on

DOWN
1. Yourself
2. Observation
3. Bundles of documents
4. Vacation resort ranch
5. Consumer
6. Brown-capped boletus mushroom
7. Dropsy
8. Past tense of bid
9. Beasts of burden
10. Cots
12. Periods of history
17. Dressed to the -. Smartly dressed
19. Doomed
21. Eyeliner powder
22. Capital of Western Samoa
23. Pen-name
26. Normal
28. Pennant
29. Pool
30. W.A. eucalypt
32. S-bends
37. Prefix, over
40. Fertile desert spot
42. Australian super-model
43. Fungus used in making soy sauce
44. - Khayyam
45. Hoarfrost
46. Roused
48. Freeze
50. - de Janeiro
51. Lair

Puzzle 47

Puzzle 48

43. Juniper
46. Goblin
47. Aztec temple
49. Angered
52. Food scrap
53. Marine hazard
54. Garden tool
55. "The Raven" author
56. Numerous
57. Even (poet.)

DOWN
1. Laboratory
2. I have
3. Physicist, Albert -
4. Disappearing
5. Smart - , show-off
6. Sexless things
7. Nick
8. Hip bones
9. Monetary unit
10. Practitioner of yoga
12. Bristle
17. Faithful
19. Yoko -
21. Skinny
22. Hawaiian honeycreeper
23. Make solemn
26. Island (France)
28. Mosaic pieces
29. Egg-shaped
30. Short dress
32. Of Salian Franks
37. Twosome
40. Remove weapons from
42. Islamic chieftain
43. Halt
44. Prefix, air
45. Ballot
46. Valley
48. Meadow
50. Supplement existence
51. Lair

ACROSS
1. Falsehood
4. Conceited
8. Gelid
11. Rent-a-car company
13. Singer
14. Zodiac sign
15. Prefix, well
16. Very young bird
18. Impassive
20. Raccoonlike carnivore
21. Giants
23. Timid
24. Hasten
25. U.S. State
27. Small particle
31. Certainly
33. Sick
34. Son of Jacob and Leah
35. One of Columbus's ships
36. Require
38. Japanese word of respect
39. Haul
41. Breakfast mixture of grains, fruit, and nuts

Puzzle 49

ACROSS
1. America (Abbr)
4. Empty
8. Mineral spring
11. Time unit
13. Church recess
14. Embrace
15. Rage
16. Foliaceous
18. Grecian architectural style
20. Young eel
21. Floated through air
23. An age
24. Revised form of Esperanto
25. Children's book author
27. Naked
31. Challenge
33. Golf peg
34. Unique thing
35. U.S. TV award
36. Jaguarundi
38. Sack
39. Colour
41. Male professional escort

43. Perchlike game fish
46. Biblical king
47. Allergic reaction substance
49. Speech impediment
52. Pastry item
53. Secular
54. Precious
55. Weep
56. Agile
57. Female deer

DOWN
1. Television frequency
2. Former coin of France
3. Ear-shaped
4. Authenticated
5. Oil cartel
6. Mount - , N.W. Qld. mining town
7. Delay
8. Switchblade
9. Vomit
10. Maturing agent
12. Indian peasant
17. Grassy plain
19. Beak
21. Broad
22. First man
23. Urgent crisis
26. U-turn (Colloq)
28. Incorporeal
29. Trade agreement
30. Therefore
32. Eagle's nest
37. Atmosphere
40. Noblemen
42. Valuable metal
43. Headwear
44. Potpourri
45. A bubble
46. Scion
48. Hiatus
50. Cracker biscuit
51. Prefix, before

Puzzle 50

ACROSS
1. Prompt
4. Suffix, skin
8. Beer
11. Second-hand
13. A Great Lake
14. British, a fool
15. Naked
16. Winemaker
18. Norwegian dramatist
20. Roman goddess of the moon
21. Catamite
23. Hallucinogenic drug
24. Anger
25. First class (1-3)
27. Minor oath
31. Urn
33. Flax ball
34. Indian queen
35. Otherwise
36. Gaelic
38. Sexless things
39. Radiation unit
41. Containing uranium
43. Tartan
46. Sea eagles
47. Salt of racemic acid
49. Paddles
52. Supplement existence
53. Object of worship
54. Russian no
55. Your (Colloq)
56. Swank
57. Secret agent

DOWN
1. Young bear
2. America (Abbr)
3. Weirdness
4. Grew
5. Ireland
6. Outfit
7. Repairs
8. Taj Mahal site
9. King of the beasts
10. Sicilian volcano
12. Debutantes
17. Downy duck
19. Large body of water
21. Donate
22. European mountain range
23. Without haste
26. And not
28. Contradicts
29. Against
30. Circular plate
32. Weird
37. Sea eagle
40. Own to
42. Great age
43. Victim
44. Tarn
45. The maple
46. English college
48. Fuss
50. Corded fabric
51. Pig enclosure

Puzzle 51

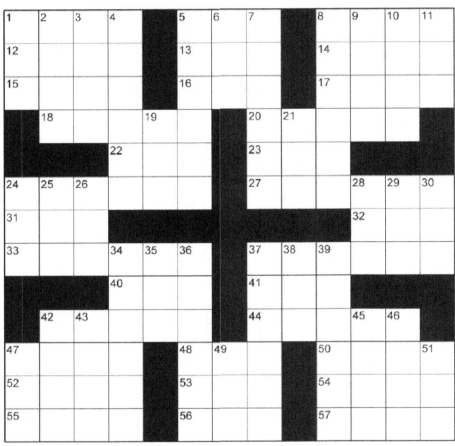

ACROSS
1. Stringed instrument
5. Clumsy person
8. Charts
12. Indian nursemaid
13. 17th letter of the Greek alphabet
14. Otherwise
15. Shout
16. Braggart (Colloq) (1.2)
17. Pause
18. Fruit pips
20. Decree
22. Prefix, the earth
23. Prefix, not
24. Sailors
27. Pastil
31. Everything
32. An age
33. Cedes
37. Swallowed
40. U-turn (Colloq)
41. Mount - , N.W. Qld. mining town
42. Explosive devices
44. African tribe
47. Point of hook
48. Label
50. Manage
52. Killer whale
53. Before
54. Personalities
55. Growl
56. Greeted
57. Rave

DOWN
1. Cattle fodder
2. Affirmative votes
3. Death rattle
4. Mucus
5. Prayer
6. Exclamation of surprise
7. Instigate
8. Sheep variety
9. Smart - , show-off
10. Surreptitious, attention getting sound
11. Become firm
19. Scottish river
21. Beetle
24. Utter
25. Biblical high priest
26. Beer
28. Brown-capped boletus mushroom
29. Gardening tool
30. Finish
34. Pertaining to the loin
35. Debutante
36. Method
37. Gallows
38. America (Abbr)
39. Cavalryman
42. Farm shed
43. Killer whale
45. Roman garment
46. On top of
47. Mire
49. Land measure
51. Superlative suffix

Puzzle 52

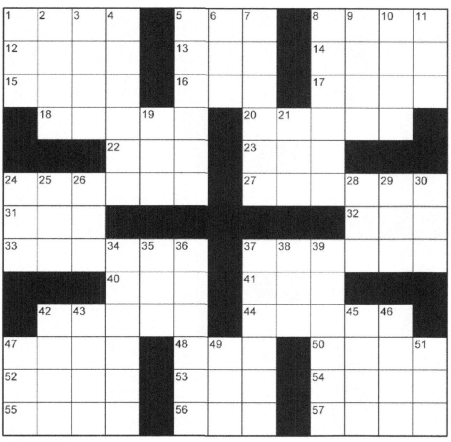

48. Mountain pass
50. Appear threateningly
52. Ancient Peruvian
53. Before
54. Sicilian volcano
55. Lighting gas
56. Become firm
57. Rice wine

DOWN
1. Newt
2. Incursion
3. Olio
4. Short stories
5. Delighted
6. Top card
7. Rogue
8. Befall
9. Against
10. Youths
11. Carp-like fish
19. Fish eggs
21. Poem
24. Marry
25. Go wrong
26. Black bird
28. British rule in India
29. Greek letter
30. Lair
34. Roman god of fire
35. Abstract being
36. Female relatives
37. Lavatory
38. 17th letter of the
    Greek alphabet
39. Large quantities
42. Unit of force
43. Remarkable
45. Jot
46. Hit on head
47. Transgress
49. Crude mineral
51. Actress, - West

ACROSS
1. Gaelic
5. Jolt
8. Indonesian resort island
12. Solid oils
13. Wood sorrel
14. Minor oath
15. Binds
16. Affirmative response
17. Ocean fluctuation
18. Midget
20. Items of currency
22. Yourself

23. Sum
24. Stoat
27. Ogled
31. Sea eagle
32. Dined
33. Taken by car
37. Native of Troy
40. Prefix, one
41. Exclamation of surprise
42. Edible red seaweed
44. Containing iodine
47. Synchronize

Puzzle 53

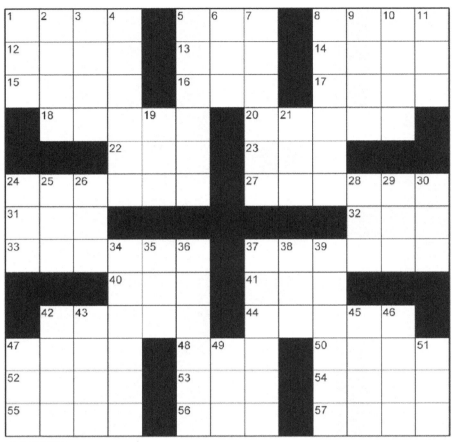

47. Land measure
48. Doctrine
50. Freshwater duck
52. City in NW France
53. Sheltered side
54. Eye part
55. Former
56. Yes
57. Thin rope

DOWN
1. Sum
2. Ring of bells
3. Hip bones
4. Clover
5. Item of footwear
6. Beer
7. Close hands tightly
8. Angel
9. Food
10. Ritual
11. Bullfight call
19. Fish eggs
21. Crude mineral
24. Groove
25. Abstract being
26. Hasten
28. Sunbeam
29. The self
30. A swelling
34. Skill
35. Mineral spring
36. Weirdly
37. Black Sea peninsular
38. Assist
39. Originating in the mind
42. Old injury mark
43. Crude minerals
45. Prefix, air
46. Den
47. Top card
49. Witness
51. Hallucinogenic drug

ACROSS
1. Capital of Western Samoa
5. Cyst envelope
8. King mackerel
12. Small valley
13. Everything
14. Greet
15. Speaking platform
16. Born
17. Suffix, diminutive
18. Scottish lord
20. Scandinavian
22. Hawaiian acacia

23. French vineyard
24. Fit new bank parts to
   shoe
27. Semitic language
31. Prefix, one
32. Mature
33. Sleeping sickness fly
37. Gorge
40. Primate
41. - de Janeiro
42. Of the sun
44. Perfect

47. Land measure
48. Doctrine
50. Freshwater duck
52. City in NW France
53. Sheltered side
54. Eye part
55. Former
56. Yes
57. Thin rope

DOWN
1. Sum
2. Ring of bells
3. Hip bones
4. Clover
5. Item of footwear
6. Beer
7. Close hands tightly
8. Angel
9. Food
10. Ritual
11. Bullfight call
19. Fish eggs
21. Crude mineral
24. Groove
25. Abstract being
26. Hasten
28. Sunbeam
29. The self
30. A swelling
34. Skill
35. Mineral spring
36. Weirdly
37. Black Sea peninsular
38. Assist
39. Originating in the mind
42. Old injury mark
43. Crude minerals
45. Prefix, air
46. Den
47. Top card
49. Witness
51. Hallucinogenic drug

Puzzle 54

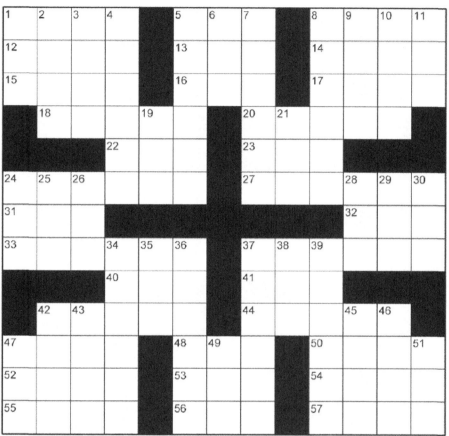

ACROSS
1. Large African antelope
5. Person steering boat and directing rowers
8. Beaten by tennis service
12. Nautical call
13. Room within a harem
14. Death rattle
15. Cut down
16. Soldiers
17. Stubborn animal
18. Cub leader
20. Spry
22. Singer, - "King" Cole
23. Owing
24. Garment's arm covering
27. Tacit
31. Conger
32. Court
33. Inclined head
37. Christian creed
40. Dined
41. I have
42. Mountain lions
44. Power line tower
47. Hamlet
48. Extrasensory perception
50. Dash
52. Fencing sword
53. Female ruff
54. Split
55. Back
56. Small amount
57. Stringed toy

DOWN
1. Clumsy person
2. Ostrich-like bird
3. Egg part
4. Benzene
5. Tufted
6. Poem
7. Place of contentment
8. Military organizations
9. Hood-like membrane
10. Australian super-model
11. Scottish river
19. Lavatory (Colloq)
21. Firearm
24. Monetary unit of Japan
25. Zodiac sign
26. Antiquity
28. Reverential fear
29. Charged particle
30. Female deer
34. More moist
35. Greek letter
36. Abandon
37. Pinched
38. Climbing plant
39. Salad vegetable
42. Pontiff
43. Fertiliser
45. Potpourri
46. Marine defence unit
47. The (German)
49. Large body of water
51. Prefix, new

Puzzle 55

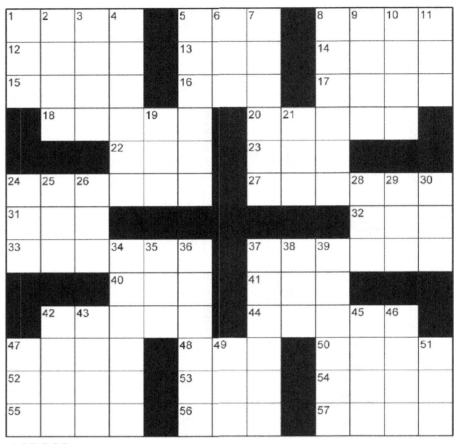

ACROSS
1. Tiller
5. Blend
8. Root of the taro
12. Fertiliser
13. Crude mineral
14. Blackbird
15. Pith
16. Beak
17. Lost blood
18. Chemical compound
20. Eagle's nest
22. The self
23. Coral island
24. Provide with feathers
27. Earlier
31. Money (Slang)
32. Bullfight call
33. Base
37. Small necktie
40. First woman
41. Prefix, over
42. Mothers
44. Weird
47. Insect feeler
48. Feline
50. Lazy
52. Send out
53. Shoemaker's tool
54. Close to
55. Guns (Slang)
56. Sheltered side
57. Work group

DOWN
1. Embrace
2. A Great Lake
3. Minus
4. Thickly entangled
5. 5th president of the U.S
6. Anger
7. Mediterranean vessels
8. Foetus
9. Delicatessen
10. Endure
11. Aged
19. Ovum
21. Legendary emperor of China
24. Watch pocket
25. Card game
26. Newt
28. Negating word
29. Biblical high priest
30. Female ruff
34. Seduces
35. Eggs
36. Peyote
37. Insect
38. Open
39. Fitting with cables
42. Mother
43. Got down from mount
45. Notion
46. Dash
47. Wooden pin
49. Reverential fear
51. Work unit

Puzzle 56

44. Republic in W Africa
47. Elite
48. Possess
50. Style
52. Train track
53. Tiny
54. Paradise
55. Church recess
56. Some
57. Lairs

DOWN
1. Garbage can
2. Enough
3. Colour of unbleached linen
4. Norwegian arctic explorer
5. Game bird
6. French, water
7. Innumerable
8. Popular drama of Japan
9. Sewing case
10. Nautical, left
11. Little devil
19. Torrid
21. And not
24. Cove
25. 17th letter of the Greek alphabet
26. Paddle
28. Consume
29. Sister
30. Attempt
34. To tickle
35. Biblical high priest
36. Waltz
37. U.S. film actor
38. Expression of disgust
39. Bored out
42. Lowest high tide
43. Egyptian goddess of fertility
45. Knob
46. Capital of Yemen
47. Brassiere
49. A swelling
51. Abstract being

ACROSS
1. "Has - ". Person who once was
5. Jewel
8. French military cap
12. Ancient Peruvian
13. Sunbeam
14. Small particle
15. Scandinavian Fate
16. Of us
17. Belch
18. Chinese martial arts
20. Eskimo

22. Greek goddess of the dawn
23. Very good (1-2)
24. Jane Eyre author, Charlotte -
27. Most parched
31. Exclamation of surprise
32. Atmosphere
33. Type of cricket delivery
37. Respectful bow
40. Island (France)
41. Mature
42. Lustrous

Puzzle 57

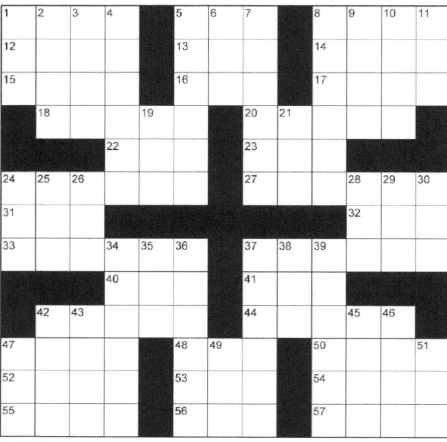

ACROSS
1. Effervesce
5. Monetary unit of Albania
8. Extinct bird
12. Region
13. Reverential fear
14. Minor oath
15. Harvest
16. Yes
17. Advance money
18. Writing tablet
20. Adores
22. Rocky peak
23. First woman
24. Thin people
27. Interweave
31. Exclamation of surprise
32. Sicken
33. Cared for
37. Deadened
40. Your (Colloq)
41. Beer
42. Baron
44. Articles
47. In bed

48. The sun
50. Leather whip
52. Republic in W Africa
53. That woman
54. Hawaiian feast
55. Of urine
56. 10th letter of the Hebrew alphabet
57. Exclamation of fright

DOWN
1. Distant
2. Angers
3. Enthusiasm
4. Mexican revolutionist
5. Strata
6. Female sheep
7. German astronomer
8. Dug
9. Double curve
10. Levels of karate proficiency
11. Rum
19. To clothe
21. Eggs
24. Took a seat
25. - Guevara
26. Fled
28. Skilled
29. Falsehood
30. Antiquity
34. Pertaining to the number 2
35. Even (poet.)
36. Stylish
37. Hammered in spikes
38. Last month
39. Fittingly
42. Type of automatic gear selector (1-3)
43. Prefix, sun
45. Island in central Hawaii
46. Exchange
47. Atomic mass unit
49. Exclamation of surprise
51. Take to court

Puzzle 58

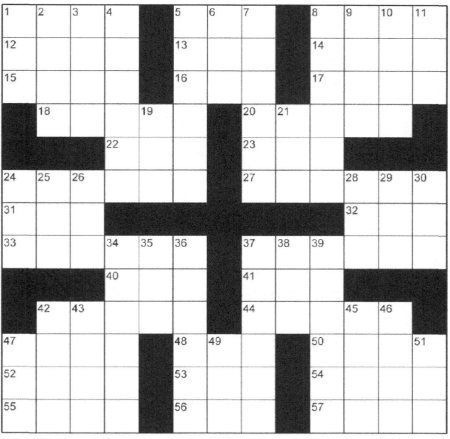

48. Policeman
50. Reclined
52. Mysterious symbol
53. Black bird
54. Weary
55. Leading player
56. Colour
57. Prefix, eight

DOWN
1. Brown shade
2. Epic poetry
3. Thailand
4. Food paste
5. Seraglios
6. Island (France)
7. Lapwing
8. Stabbing weapon
9. Hip bones
10. Oven
11. Greek letter
19. - Vegas, US gambling city
21. Climbing plant
24. Sailor
25. Not
26. Newt
28. Exclamation of surprise
29. Henpeck
30. A couple
34. Safari member
35. Superlative suffix
36. East Indies sailor
37. Nest-building wasp
38. Family
39. Theater district
42. Solicit
43. Sicilian volcano
45. Secular
46. Soil
47. Missus
49. Monad
51. Prefix, new

ACROSS
1. Trial
5. Coxa
8. Levee
12. Capital of Western Samoa
13. Beer
14. Got down from mount
15. Ark builder
16. Female ruff
17. Venomous lizard
18. Grin
20. Canvas-like fabric
22. Vietnam

23. I have
24. Metamorphic rock
27. Despot
31. Clumsy person
32. Utterance of hesitation
33. Sanctuary
37. Shrew
40. America (Abbr)
41. Biblical high priest
42. Camp shelters
44. Scandinavian poet
47. Clump of trees

Puzzle 59

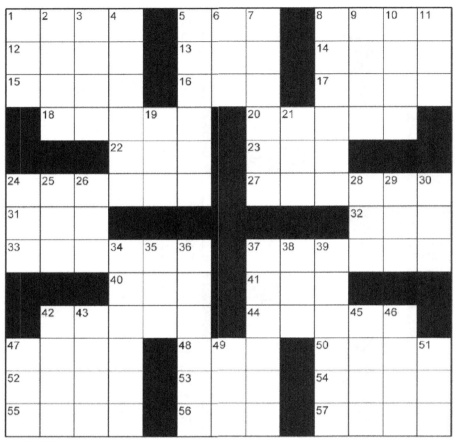

44. Nest
47. Water craft
48. Eggs
50. Angered
52. Root of the taro
53. Battle
54. Minor oath
55. Achieve
56. Pig enclosure
57. Dispatched

DOWN
1. Small long-haired dog
2. Praise
3. Former Soviet Union
4. Stable
5. Fisherman
6. Expire
7. Catchword
8. Rates
9. Nobleman
10. Nervous
11. Prefix, new
19. Tiny
21. Island (France)
24. Hotel
25. Sheltered side
26. Affirmative vote
28. Spread out for drying
29. Actor, - Chaney
30. Superlative suffix
34. German
35. Meadow
36. Arm joints
37. Consisting of nine
38. Biblical high priest
39. Whirlpools
42. Alkali
43. Muslim judge
45. Incite
46. - Connery
47. Plead
49. Large tub
51. Once common, now
    banned, insecticide

ACROSS
1. In addition to
5. Commercials
8. Valley
12. Kiln for drying hops
13. Zero
14. Travelled on
15. Ponder
16. Prefix, the earth
17. Jason's ship
18. Lingering manner of
    speaking
20. Dizzy

22. Scottish river
23. Beer
24. Actor
27. Snuggle
31. U-turn (Colloq)
32. Greek goddess of the
    dawn
33. Insect
37. Contraction of need not
40. Conger
41. Aged
42. Nestling pigeon

Puzzle 60

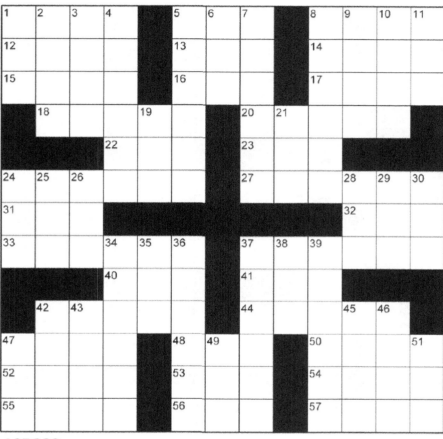

48. An age
50. Roman dates
52. Persian lord
53. Young goat
54. Break suddenly
55. Mongol tent
56. Ethnic telecaster
57. Monetary unit of Western Samoa

DOWN
1. Brassiere
2. U.S. State
3. Advance money
4. Going out with
5. Gasped
6. 17th letter of the Greek alphabet
7. Birds of prey
8. An Australian
9. Sea eagle
10. Back
11. Synthetic yttrium aluminum garnet
19. Witness
21. Bullfight call
24. Free
25. America (Abbr)
26. Girl (Slang)
28. Owing
29. Superlative suffix
30. Scottish river
34. Undeveloped
35. Reverential fear
36. Barracouta (Plural)
37. Fears greatly
38. Otic organ
39. Lyric poet
42. Island of Hawaii
43. Leading player
45. Dame - Everage, Humphries' character
46. Trade agreement
47. Firmament
49. Chest bone
51. Mineral spring

ACROSS
1. Daring
5. Prefix, before
8. Ethereal
12. Ostrich-like bird
13. Exclamation of surprise
14. Fertiliser
15. Isn't
16. Egg drink
17. Catch
18. Writer of lyric poetry
20. The one defeated
22. Born
23. Biblical high priest
24. Craggy
27. Sowed
31. Mount - , N.W. Qld. mining town
32. Avail of
33. Texas city
37. Erase
40. Grain beard
41. Sunbeam
42. Prefix, bone
44. Went wrong
47. Cloy

Puzzle 61

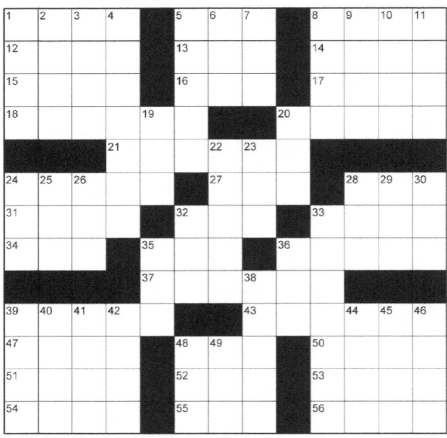

48. Last letter
50. Exclamation of fright
51. Team
52. Anger
53. Region
54. Front of ship
55. Normal
56. Skin

DOWN
1. Ululate
2. In this place
3. Angers
4. Small amount
5. Small yeast-raised pancake
6. Charged particle
7. Operations (colloq)
8. Leading player
9. Pith helmet
10. A Great Lake
11. Legumes
19. Breakfast cereal
20. Question
22. Jolly - , Pirate's flag
23. Arrest
24. Brassiere
25. Greek goddess of the dawn
26. Exclamation of surprise
28. Cove
29. Eggs
30. Unit of loudness
32. Relation
33. Command to a horse
35. Top pupil
36. Fled
38. Downy duck
39. Lock part fitted to staple
40. Primordial giant in Norse myth
41. Repeat
42. Once again
44. Ireland
45. Fencing sword
46. Trade agreement
48. Toothed fastener
49. An age

ACROSS
1. A fancy
5. Prefix, life
8. Pace
12. Prefix, air
13. Cut off
14. Ripped
15. Angered
16. - and outs, intricacies
17. Capital of Western Samoa
18. A sore
20. Zodiac sign
21. Piles of stones
24. Beautiful

27. Large tree
28. Curtsy
31. Wander
32. Russian secret police
33. Donated
34. Fire remains
35. Expire
36. Monetary unit of Saudi Arabia
37. Not perused
39. Dassie
43. In fact
47. Prayer ending

Puzzle 62

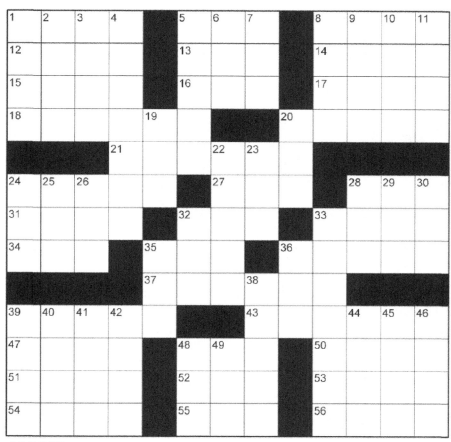

ACROSS
1. Tubular pasta in short pieces
5. Cove
8. Lustreless
12. Potpourri
13. Prefix, over
14. Double curve
15. Charge over property
16. Pet form of Leonard
17. Trundle
18. Antenna
20. Fireplace
21. Outlays
24. Small isle
27. An age
28. Unit of loudness
31. Therefore
32. U-turn (Colloq)
33. Large volume
34. Gender
35. W.A. river
36. Capital of Tibet
37. In any case
39. Intended
43. River in W central Africa
47. Indian currency
48. My, French (Plural)
50. Thoroughfare
51. Many
52. Bitter vetch
53. British National Gallery
54. Monetary unit of Angola
55. Attempt
56. Eldest son of Noah

DOWN
1. French novelist
2. Tennis star, - Natase
3. Row
4. Changes into ions
5. Reigning beauty
6. Primate
7. - and Yang
8. Morning
9. Eager
10. Inform
11. Prefix, distant
19. Fitting
20. Mount - , N.W. Qld. mining town
22. Indigent
23. Arid
24. Sexless things
25. That woman
26. Unit of illumination
28. Large snake
29. Printer's measures
30. Meadow
32. Vase
33. Frustrates (a purpose)
35. Breakfast cereal
36. Throw lightly
38. Lewd woman
39. Shopping centre
40. Enough
41. Poker stake
42. Malay rice dish, - goreng
44. Ark builder
45. Fence opening
46. As previously given
48. Greeted
49. Go wrong

Puzzle 63

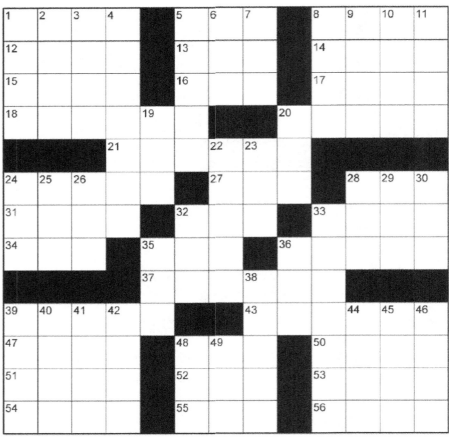

47. Greasy
48. Monetary unit of Vietnam
50. Remedy
51. Migrant farm worker
52. Commercials
53. Poems
54. Devices for fishing
55. Cooking implement
56. Nipple

DOWN
1. Refuse
2. Auricular
3. Cotton seed vessel
4. Reacted to hay fever
5. Mediterranean island
6. Be indebted
7. Scottish river
8. Hit hard
9. Prefix, eight
10. Exhibit
11. Cure
19. Domesticated animal
20. Pig enclosure
22. Capital of Tibet
23. Clumsy person
24. Egyptian serpent
25. That woman
26. Male offspring
28. Israeli submachine gun
29. Cyst envelope
30. Some
32. Room within a harem
33. Stone fruit
35. Island (France)
36. Large body of water
38. Spook
39. Anon
40. Spear point
41. Got down from mount
42. Stains
44. Naked
45. Region
46. Nidus
48. Comforter or quilt
49. Fuss

ACROSS
1. Tells on
5. Very modern
8. Nonsense
12. English college
13. Reverential fear
14. Pain
15. African river
16. Sheltered side
17. Portico
18. Named
20. Shoulder wrap
21. Fanatic
24. Thing of value
27. Cattle fodder
28. America (Abbr)
31. Fitted with shoes
32. Clumsy person
33. Islamic call to prayer
34. Female swan
35. Egos
36. Savoury
37. Encampment
39. Digging tool
43. Island in the South China Sea

Puzzle 64

ACROSS
1. Offers a price
5. Edge
8. Surreptitious, attention getting sound
12. Heed
13. Land measure
14. Vow
15. Never
16. Knowledge
17. Double curve
18. Die
20. Developed
21. Having nodes
24. Renounce
27. Hive insect
28. A charge
31. Hautboy
32. Meadow
33. Morning
34. Castrated male cat
35. Meadow
36. - Rock, Uluru
37. Breathe in
39. Young of the dog
43. Catlike
47. Jot
48. Breakfast cereal
50. Unique thing
51. Drunkards
52. Open
53. Inflammation (Suffix)
54. Supplements
55. That woman
56. Apportion

DOWN
1. Skeletal part
2. Mountain goat
3. Profound
4. Cleansing injection
5. Gathered up grass cuttings
6. Anger
7. Soldiers
8. Indigent
9. Palm starch
10. Olio
11. At that time
19. Kangaroo
20. Horse command
22. Belief involving sorcery
23. Large body of water
24. Thick mist
25. Japanese sash
26. Hold up
28. Enemy
29. Go wrong
30. Abstract being
32. Pet form of Leonard
33. Pertaining to the spinal cord
35. Mouth part
36. Beer
38. Later
39. Sensible
40. Crook
41. Suffix, diminutive
42. Girl
44. Towards the centre
45. - Armstrong, first man on moon
46. Gaelic
48. Exclamation of wonder
49. Primate

Puzzle 65

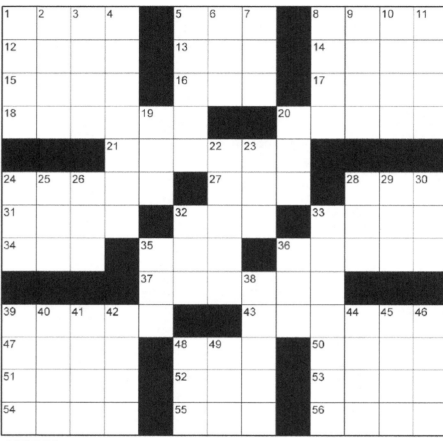

43. Ten year period
47. On top of
48. Highest mountain in Crete
50. Drag
51. Valley
52. A delay
53. Periods of history
54. One's parents (Colloq)
55. Soap ingredient
56. Advise

DOWN
1. Measure of medicine
2. Roman poet
3. Son of Jacob and Leah
4. Deletion
5. Monetary unit of France
6. Exclamation of surprise
7. Scale note
8. Political combine
9. American grey wolf
10. Ireland
11. Moistens
19. Open
20. Sexless things
22. Leaning
23. Top cricket hit
24. To silence
25. Biblical high priest
26. Prefix, not
28. Metal rod
29. Biblical high priest
30. Not
32. Greeted
33. Instructor
35. Bend
36. Female sheep
38. Maxim
39. Accolade
40. Iridescent gem
41. Informed
42. Single items
44. River in central Switzerland
45. Couple
46. Otherwise
48. Sick
49. Time of sunshine

ACROSS
1. Apportion
5. A craze
8. Gusted
12. Finished
13. 17th letter of the Greek alphabet
14. Tradition
15. Hindu god of destruction
16. Exclamation of surprise
17. Funeral notice
18. US electronics inventor, Thomas -
20. Images

21. Directed upward
24. Genus
27. It is
28. Scottish hill
31. Agave
32. Blend
33. Monetary unit of Western Samoa
34. Rummy game
35. Unit of loudness
36. Weird
37. Capital of Canada
39. Obsequious act

Puzzle 66

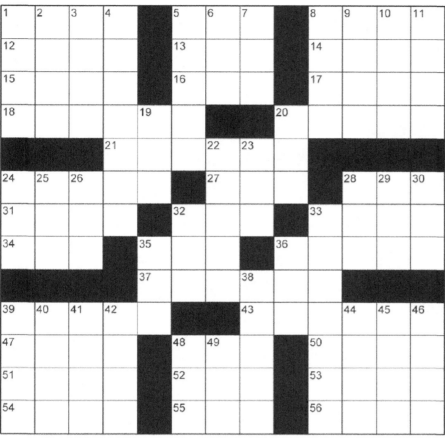

ACROSS
1. Gust
5. Sister
8. Record conversation
12. Thick cord
13. New Zealand bird
14. Maturing agent
15. Days before
16. Tavern
17. Capital of Shaanxi province, China
18. Drink of the gods
20. Fluid measures
21. Portable ice-boxes
24. Flies high
27. Prefix, three
28. Sulky
31. Ache
32. Once existed
33. An appointment
34. Limb
35. Indian dish
36. Body of deputised hunters
37. In any case
39. Take sounding
43. Proverbs

47. Lively
48. Fruit conserve
50. Ancient Teuton
51. Ritual
52. Eggs
53. Sea eagle
54. Redact
55. Unit of loudness
56. Quantity of paper

DOWN
1. Machine-gun
2. Adore
3. Oil cartel
4. Situated in the west
5. Grin
6. Charged particle
7. Japanese word of respect
8. Cab
9. Against
10. Bog fuel
11. Sea eagles
19. Donkey
20. Pressure symbol
22. Mediterranean country
23. Bitter vetch
24. Mineral spring
25. Paddle
26. Intention
28. Vapour
29. Sexless things
30. Horse command
32. Ashen
33. Widow
35. Skilled
36. Seed vessel
38. Porter
39. Funeral fire
40. Reposed
41. Upper respiratory tract infection
42. Greet
44. Pierce with horn
45. Sicilian volcano
46. Eldest son of Noah
48. Task
49. Greeting

Puzzle 67

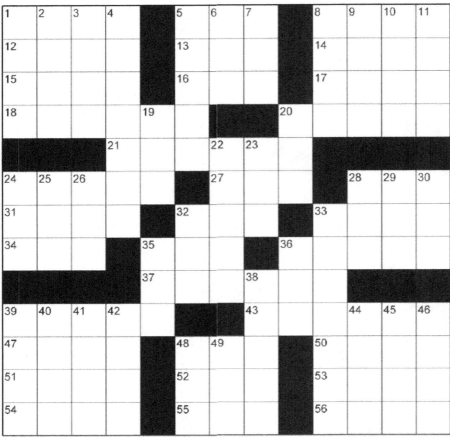

ACROSS
1. Split
5. Mother
8. Style
12. Region
13. Mount - , N.W. Qld. mining town
14. Fencing sword
15. Row
16. Skilled
17. Shopping centre
18. Apocrypha book
20. Lounges
21. Wholly

24. Summoned
27. Hold up
28. Charged particle
31. Mimicked
32. Metal rod
33. Indian currency
34. Scottish river
35. Part of a circle
36. Beginning
37. Elephant keeper
39. Representation of the Buddha
43. Proverbs

47. Opera solo
48. Sea (French)
50. Republic in the Caribbean
51. Police informer
52. Crude mineral
53. Press clothes
54. Australian super-model
55. Evil
56. Immerse in water

DOWN
1. Assess
2. Eye part
3. Give food to
4. Loitered
5. Amid
6. America (Abbr)
7. Fairy queen
8. Brief note
9. Iridescent gem
10. Small valley
11. Long fish
19. Also
20. Throw lightly
22. Mountain spinach
23. Rocky peak
24. Cushion
25. Primate
26. Horse command
28. - and outs, intricacies
29. Monad
30. Singer, - "King" Cole
32. Brassiere
33. Medicine neutralising stomach acidity
35. Atomic mass unit
36. Musical instrument
38. Rowed
39. Curse
40. European mountain range
41. Rotate
42. Rice wine
44. Hindu teacher
45. Black
46. Subsided
48. Unruly crowd
49. An age

Puzzle 68

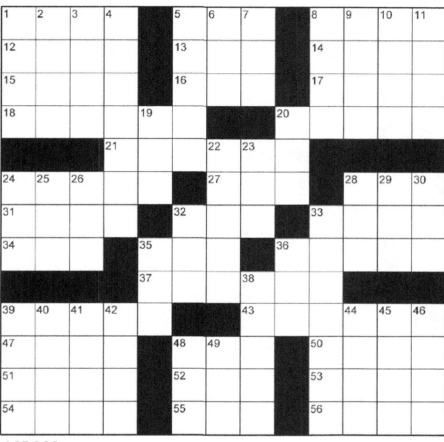

47. Paddles
48. Governor
50. Parasitic insect
51. Clarified butter
52. Black bird
53. Supplements
54. Took legal action against
55. Sister
56. Moist

DOWN
1. Subsided
2. Dash
3. Mother of Apollo
4. Dancer's one-peice costume
5. Republic in N Africa
6. America (Abbr)
7. Needlefish
8. Chain armour
9. Egg-shaped
10. Business emblem
11. Enough
19. An explosive
20. Electrical unit
22. Father
23. Printer's measures
24. - Guevara
25. Monetary unit of Vietnam
26. Abstract being
28. Biblical high priest
29. Regret
30. Go wrong
32. Exclamation of surprise
33. Mocked
35. Rotational speed
36. Sick
38. Jeans
39. Large tree remnants
40. Island of Hawaii
41. American Indian
42. Second-hand
44. Every
45. Appear
46. Lock part fitted to staple
48. Vapour
49. Prefix, one

ACROSS
1. Vend
5. Haul
8. Breakwater
12. To the sheltered side
13. Mount - , N.W. Qld. mining town
14. Shakespeare's river
15. Western pact
16. Metal rod
17. The villain in Othello
18. Tangled
20. Permit
21. Head garland
24. Flint
27. Electrical unit
28. Before
31. Arm extremity
32. Commercials
33. Elide
34. Greek goddess of the dawn
35. Radiation unit
36. More gelid
37. Tissue-thin layers of pastry
39. Relieving doctor
43. Small and mischievous

Puzzle 69

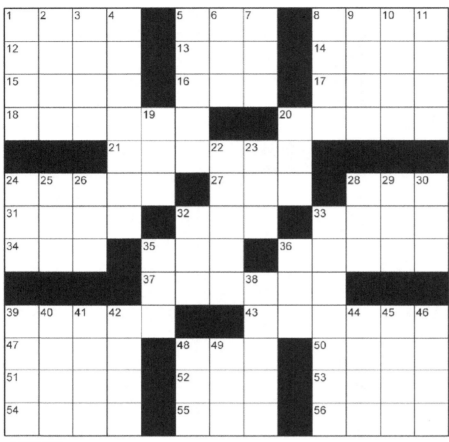

48. Normal
50. Notion
51. Brink
52. Revised form of Esperanto
53. Groom hair
54. Ceases living
55. Greek goddess of the dawn
56. Greek goddess of strife

DOWN
1. Moslem demon
2. Fertiliser
3. Malay rice dish, - goreng
4. Put in bondage
5. Extremely modest person
6. Affirmative vote
7. Time of sunshine
8. Ambition
9. Official language of Pakistan
10. The maple
11. Hindu lawgiver
19. Supplement existence
20. America (Abbr)
22. Ogles
23. Part of a circle
24. In favour of
25. Uncooked
26. Open
28. Mountain pass
29. Poem
30. Fox
32. Weep
33. Chickadees
35. Skilled
36. An explosive
38. Wallaroos
39. Toboggan
40. Muslim judge
41. Incite
42. Roman dates
44. Scent
45. Prefix, part
46. Labels
48. Pastry item
49. Fuss

ACROSS
1. Sixth month of the year
5. Cushion
8. Pacific island U.S. naval base
12. Republic in SW Asia
13. Handwoven Scandinavian rug
14. Killer whale
15. Scottish headland
16. U-turn (Colloq)
17. Capital of Yemen
18. Hammered in spikes
20. Ayers Rock
21. Cub leaders

24. Verify
27. An age
28. Infant's bed
31. Take by force
32. Dry (wine)
33. Bustle or fuss (Colloq) (2-2)
34. Be indebted
35. Beetle
36. Covered with ceramic pieces
37. Away
39. Small firework
43. Extreme
47. Fat

Puzzle 70

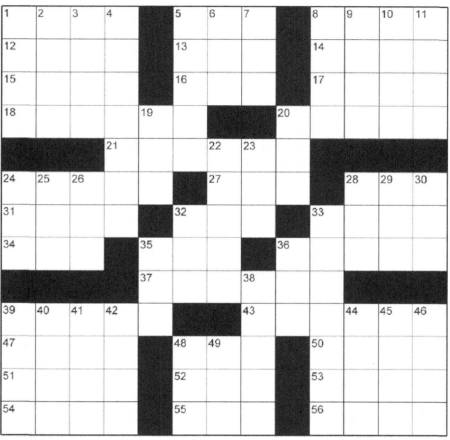

48. Greek letter
50. Hire
51. Cloistered women
52. Sicken
53. Suffix, diminutive
54. Minor oath
55. Raises
56. Arab vessel

DOWN
1. Act silently
2. Second-hand
3. Pennant
4. Pert. to a union of states
5. Humiliate
6. Weir
7. Annihilate
8. A legume
9. Adjoin
10. Painful
11. Knot in wood
19. 17th letter of the Greek alphabet
20. Extrasensory perception
22. Cloys
23. America (Abbr)
24. Brown-capped boletus mushroom
25. Greeting
26. Spanish hero
28. Dry (wine)
29. Large tree
30. Which person
32. Antiquity
33. Strained
35. Braggart (Colloq) (1.2)
36. Crooked
38. Iridescent gems
39. Breeze
40. Time unit
41. Sicilian volcano
42. Final
44. Third son of Adam
45. Towards the centre
46. Olio
48. French, water
49. Gratuity

ACROSS
1. Handle clumsily
5. Axlike tool
8. Soak up sun
12. Small island
13. Bleat
14. Black
15. Honey liquor
16. Electrical unit
17. Subtle emanation
18. Grass trimming tools
20. Go in
21. A monkey

24. Chocolate nut
27. Egyptian serpent
28. Female pig
31. Sinister
32. Greek letter
33. Wife of Jacob
34. Prefix, foot
35. Island (France)
36. An eccentric person
37. Superficially absorb
39. Engulf
43. Suppuration
47. Jot

Puzzle 71

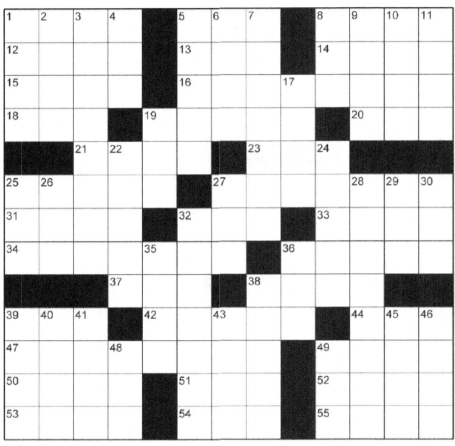

49. Forest growth
50. River in central Switzerland
51. Anger
52. High temperature
53. Indian peasant
54. Bounder
55. Root of the taro

DOWN
1. Insect feeler
2. 6th month of the Jewish calendar
3. River channel
4. Dined
5. Distributed cards
6. 12th month of the Jewish calendar
7. Broadened
8. Resinous deposit
9. Fetid
10. Compassion
11. Eye inflammation
17. Semite
19. Mount - , N.W. Qld. mining town
22. Lookers
24. Profits
25. Laboratory
26. Island (France)
27. Speck
28. Pockmarked like lunar surface
29. Auction item
30. Abstract being
32. Mental
35. Female sheep
36. Remove intestines from fish
38. Yawned
39. Distant
40. Stage show
41. Polynesian root food
43. Italian currency
45. Heavy metal
46. Derived from a ketone
48. Obtain
49. Definite article

ACROSS
1. Prefix, beyond
5. Nocturnal precipitation
8. Cuts off
12. Entrance
13. Biblical high priest
14. Got down from mount
15. Wash
16. Daring
18. Prefix, before
19. Sicker
20. Change colour of
21. Pause
23. Henpeck
25. Republic in N Africa
27. Total rout
31. To the sheltered side
32. Seed vessel
33. Press clothes
34. Prolonged rest in bed
36. Biting insects
37. Two-up
38. Sudden blow
39. Fitting
42. Applause
44. Moose
47. Main vessel of a shipping

Puzzle 72

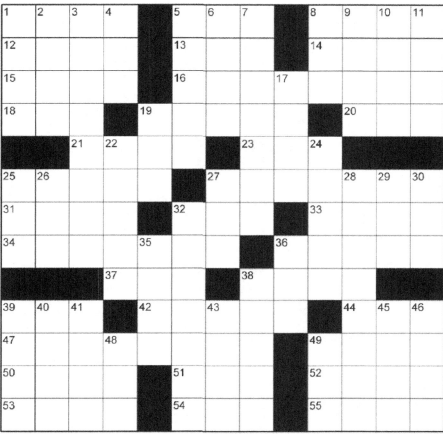

ACROSS
1. Harp-like instrument
5. Stomach
8. Insane
12. Islamic chieftain
13. Highest mountain in Crete
14. European mountain range
15. Fruit
16. Metallic element
18. Prefix, three
19. Suffix, diminutives
20. Commercials
21. Mothers
23. Knock with knuckles
25. Mangers
27. Disease associated with the eating away of limbs
31. Detest
32. Morose
33. A Great Lake
34. Charmingly simple
36. Fronded plants
37. Otic organ
38. Sea eagle
39. Definite article
42. Irish county
44. Tatter
47. Low toned singer
49. Bulk
50. Got down from mount
51. Egos
52. New Zealand parrots
53. Antarctic explorer
54. Negating word
55. Is not

DOWN
1. Departed
2. Primordial giant in Norse myth
3. Stiffness
4. Bitter vetch
5. Baseball gloves
6. Entrance
7. Irrigated
8. Firearm
9. Opera solo
10. Showy ornament
11. Charity
17. As soon as possible
19. Printer's measures
22. White poplar tree
24. Groom oneself
25. Greek letter
26. Radiation unit
27. Resinous deposit
28. Planetariums
29. Transgress
30. Affirmative response
32. Meat cut
35. Final
36. To and -
38. Excrete
39. Type of automatic gear selector (1-3)
40. Nimbus
41. Greek goddess of strife
43. Prefix, India
45. Islamic call to prayer
46. Romance tale
48. Sexless things
49. Snow runner

Puzzle 73

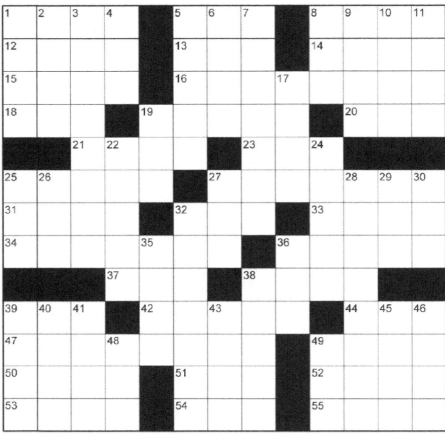

44. Beak
47. Legal status of an alien
49. Italian wine province
50. Rectangular pier
51. - de mer, seasickness
52. Glass panel
53. Frighten
54. Commercials
55. Russian emperor

DOWN
1. Old injury mark
2. Knob
3. Able to adapt
4. Normal
5. Letter cross-line
6. Opera solo
7. Person who drives a wagon
8. Small bird
9. Information
10. Sewing case
11. Pickling herb
17. Colours
19. 13th letter of the Hebrew alphabet
22. Rages
24. Based on eight
25. Island (France)
26. Weir
27. Carried out
28. State of USA
29. Born
30. Spread out for drying
32. American state
35. Great age
36. Expression of contempt
38. Scots
39. Dutch name of The Hague
40. Arm bone
41. Fragments
43. Minor oath
45. Sicilian volcano
46. Coffin stand
48. Consume
49. Fitting

ACROSS
1. Break suddenly
5. Witnessed
8. Bound
12. Musical ending
13. An age
14. Monetary unit of Peru
15. 6th month of the Jewish calendar
16. Having a just claim
18. Corded fabric
19. Mew
20. Lubricant
21. Not kosher
23. Prefix, new
25. Jargon
27. Discourse on a theme
31. Molten rock
32. Atmosphere
33. Forest growth
34. Green gem
36. Cooked in oven
37. Large body of water
38. Festival
39. Nave
42. Belief involving sorcery

Puzzle 74

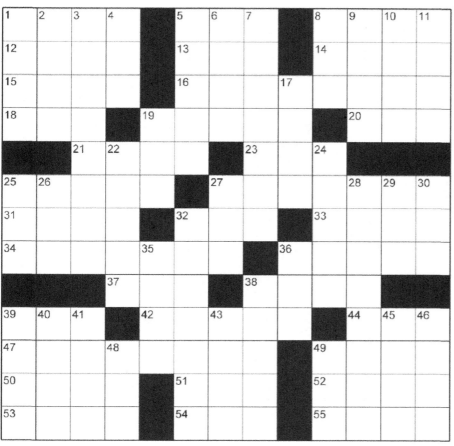

42. Boredom
44. Prefix, not
47. Celestial
49. Prefix, distant
50. South-east Asian nation
51. Writing fluid
52. Small island
53. Evict
54. Vapour
55. Russian emperor

DOWN
1. Hungarian sheepdog
2. Indigo
3. Young pike
4. Dined
5. Pale green mosslike lichen
6. Fly high
7. Put grain in silo
8. Sicken
9. Drag logs
10. Hoe-shaped axe
11. Verse
17. Great age
19. Bitter vetch
22. Turkish river
24. Stroll
25. Spider's structure
26. Affirmative vote
27. Dance step
28. Indecentness
29. Prefix, three
30. To date
32. Monetary unit of
    Germany
35. Looker
36. Greek letter
38. Acts peevishly
39. Capital of Norway
40. Hawaiian feast
41. Epic poetry
43. Grandmother
45. Earthen pot
46. Never
48. Superlative suffix
49. Small bird

ACROSS
1. Father
5. Avail of
8. As soon as possible
12. Military detachment
13. Male offspring
14. Prefix, India
15. Adult nits
16. Pronounce as a nasal
    sound
18. Family
19. Weird
20. Jewel

21. Jaguarundi
23. Cut off
25. Goods
27. Punishment
31. Sight organs
32. Cushion
33. Withered
34. Tenets
36. Lapwing
37. Soap ingredient
38. Fitted with shoes
39. Bullfight call

Puzzle 75

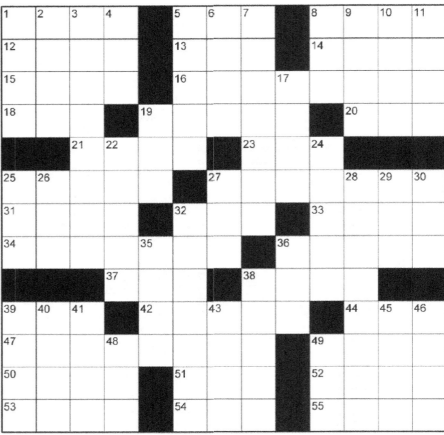

42. Storms
44. Label
47. Outdoors cooking event
49. Weary
50. Twining stem
51. Donkey
52. Italian capital
53. Toboggan
54. That woman
55. Current month

DOWN
1. Feeble
2. Capital of Norway
3. Substance for killing rats
4. Twosome
5. Remove a cap
6. Anon
7. Failure to attend
8. Expire
9. Monetary unit of Peru
10. Agitate
11. Rooster
17. Chain armour
19. Long-leaved lettuce
22. Raise (Flag)
24. Confused mixture of
    sounds
25. A couple
26. Fled
27. Fairy
28. Inference
29. Regret
30. Gender
32. Llamas
35. Ireland
36. It is
38. Large duck-like birds
39. Wanes
40. Train track
41. Sea eagle
43. Spurt forth
45. 3 Weapons
46. Root vegetable
48. Cot
49. Prefix, three

ACROSS
1. Part of speech
5. America (Abbr)
8. Circular plate
12. Son of Isaac and Rebekah
13. Jack in cribbage
14. Towards the centre
15. Singer
16. Skin preparation
18. Colorful form of the
    common carp
19. Capital of Crete
20. Vex

21. Hew
23. Pen point
25. Threesomes
27. Chocolate and cream
    delicacies
31. Dry riverbed
32. Beer
33. Sky colour
34. One's own person
36. Early form of FAX
37. Gratuity
38. Venomous lizard
39. Before

Puzzle 76

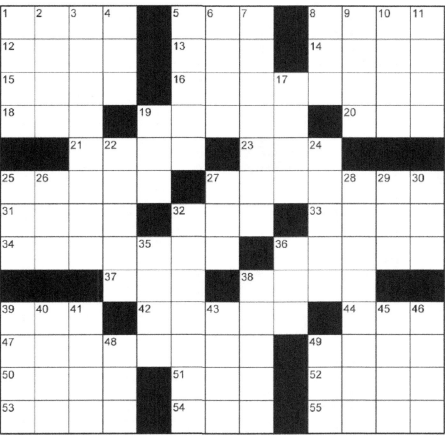

ACROSS
1. Lethargic
5. Black bird
8. Image
12. Off-Broadway theater award
13. Wood sorrel
14. Something not to be done (2-2)
15. Brown and white horse
16. Beat soundly
18. Lair
19. Equals
20. Crude mineral
21. Type of automatic gear selector (1-3)
23. Dined
25. Touches
27. Wove wool
31. Bear constellation
32. Small bird
33. Weight allowance
34. Dwelt
36. Barrier
37. Grandmother
38. Speech impediment
39. Bullfight call
42. Backs of necks
44. Exclamation of surprise
47. Device which helps make angular cuts (5.3)
49. Garden pest
50. Adolescent pimples
51. Garland
52. Assist
53. Harvest
54. Printer's measures
55. Son of Isaac and Rebekah

DOWN
1. Nobleman
2. Hautboy
3. Very large woman
4. Japanese currency
5. Person foolishly fond of another
6. Pain
7. Sanction
8. - and outs, intricacies
9. Small salmon
10. Unique thing
11. Knob
17. Italian wine province
19. Dance step
22. Inflammatory swelling
24. Suffix, diminutives
25. Animal pelt
26. Before
27. Young goat
28. Young frogs
29. Work unit
30. Scottish river
32. Defendable
35. Norseman
36. Belonging to him
38. Lexicon
39. - Khayyam
40. Adult nits
41. Sicilian volcano
43. Verse
45. Hawaiian dance
46. Russian secret police
48. Corded fabric
49. That woman

Puzzle 77

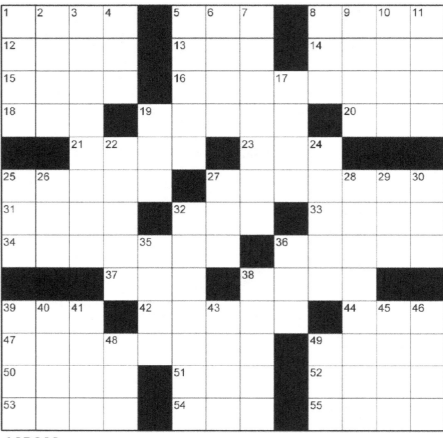

ACROSS
1. Overacts
5. Flu (Colloq)
8. Fine powder
12. Opera solo
13. Monad
14. Double curve
15. Car registration (Colloq)
16. Delivered
18. Level of karate proficiency
19. Hand out
20. Land measure
21. Evict
23. Braggart (Colloq) (1.2)

25. Contour feather
27. Moderately slow
31. Arm bone
32. Bind
33. Eyeliner powder
34. Perforated
36. Roister
37. Blend
38. Fleet rodent
39. Fire remains
42. Thatching
44. Laboratory
47. Bend

49. Bulk
50. River in central
    Switzerland
51. Boy
52. Islamic call to prayer
53. Indian peasant
54. Printer's measures
55. Repair

DOWN
1. Difficult
2. Region
3. Small and delicately pretty
4. Cracker biscuit
5. Most bad
6. Single items
7. Real
8. Pedal digit
9. Taj Mahal site
10. Ogle
11. Yield
17. Deceased
19. Mount - , N.W. Qld.
    mining town
22. Remove weapons from
24. Creator
25. Young dog
26. Biblical high priest
27. Assist
28. Put into the form of a
    novel
29. Definite article
30. Former measure of
    length
32. Woven material
35. Prehistoric sepulchral
    tomb
36. Uncooked
38. Arm extremities
39. Distant
40. Kill
41. Champion
43. Wander
45. Islamic call to prayer
46. Curve
48. Prefix, whale
49. Uncle -, USA personified

Puzzle 78

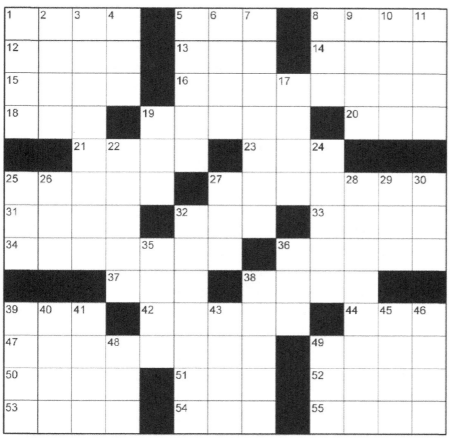

42. Cow's milk sac
44. Electrical unit
47. Announce
49. Glass bottle
50. Reverberate
51. Sweet potato
52. Ancient Peruvian
53. Arab vessel
54. Wily
55. Wan

DOWN
1. Dent
2. Dash
3. Climbing shrub
4. Yes
5. Heroic tales
6. Trial
7. Not straight
8. Card game
9. Taverns
10. Egyptian deity
11. Foot part
17. Developed
19. Mature
22. Glazing material
24. Eagle's nest
25. Actress, - Farrow
26. Shady tree
27. Soil
28. Abstains
29. Consume
30. Arid
32. Greatest times
35. First king of Israel
36. And not
38. Set with gems
39. Mimicked
40. Curved entrance
41. Laughing sound (2.2)
43. Face
45. Speed relative to the
    speed of sound
46. Stage show
48. Bovine
49. By way of

ACROSS
1. Moist with dew
5. Etcetera
8. Edges
12. Tennis star, - Natase
13. Each
14. Upon
15. U.S. space agency
16. Equiangular
18. An explosive
19. Role player
20. That woman
21. Ova

23. New Zealand parrot
25. Blackbird
27. Connected to effluent
    mains
31. Hip bones
32. Brick carrier
33. Back
34. Gathered
36. Smart
37. Utter
38. Apparently successful
    project
39. Exclamation of surprise

Puzzle 79

47. Reallocate
49. Lively
50. Jason's ship
51. Monetary unit of Romania
52. A Great Lake
53. Large snakes
54. Garland
55. Prayer ending

DOWN
1. Suffix, diminutive
2. River in central Switzerland
3. Formerly Ceylon
4. Male cat
5. Toss
6. Require
7. Despotism
8. My, French (Plural)
9. Peaks
10. Greek goddess of the earth
11. Prefix, India
17. At sea
19. The sun
22. Crypt
24. Heeds
25. Prefix, three
26. Breakfast cereal
27. Sea eagle
28. Tepid
29. Before
30. - and don'ts
32. Shipping document
35. Angers
36. Time of sunshine
38. Boredom
39. Crustacean
40. Prefix, air
41. Hindu music
43. Double curve
45. A Great Lake
46. Adolescent
48. Distress signal
49. Yes

ACROSS
1. The Orient
5. An explosive
8. The three wise men
12. Polynesian root food
13. Attention-getting call
14. Dash
15. Decorate (Xmas tree)
16. Spoke gratingly again
18. Conger
19. Ice-cream drinks
20. Cracker biscuit
21. Confess

23. Prefix, new
25. Of pitch
27. Made possible
31. Rough earthenware
32. Crooked
33. Wallaroo
34. Latin
36. Levees
37. Attempt
38. Relax
39. Automobile
42. Black wood
44. Soak

Puzzle 80

ACROSS
1. Responsibility
5. Benedictine monk's title
8. Seethe
12. Valley
13. Biblical high priest
14. Monster
15. Rectangular pier
16. Edible bean
18. New Guinea seaport
19. Evade
20. Abstract being
21. Thick cord
23. Crow call
25. Artless
27. Censure
31. Agave
32. Gelid
33. Endure
34. Level cut on hillside
36. Tam
37. 9th letter of the Hebrew alphabet
38. Basic monetary unit of Ghana
39. An age
42. Roister
44. Stay rope
47. Having parts deleted for moral purposes
49. River in central Switzerland
50. Detest
51. Highest mountain in Crete
52. Submachine gun
53. Norse god
54. Automobile
55. New Zealand parrots

DOWN
1. Egg-shaped
2. Grandmother
3. Intentionally kept concealed
4. Large body of water
5. Dig
6. Potpourri
7. Art of mimicking
8. Curtsy
9. Double curve
10. Republic in SW Asia
11. Telescope part
17. 6th month of the Jewish calendar
19. Primate
22. Open
24. Forded
25. Singer, - "King" Cole
26. Beer
27. Top card
28. Supply with water
29. Horse command
30. Seine
32. Jaundiced
35. Prefix, air
36. Unit of loudness
38. Timber tree
39. Reverberate
40. Peruse
41. Against
43. The sacred scriptures of Hinduism
45. Fertiliser
46. Desires
48. Monetary unit of Japan
49. Question

Puzzle 81

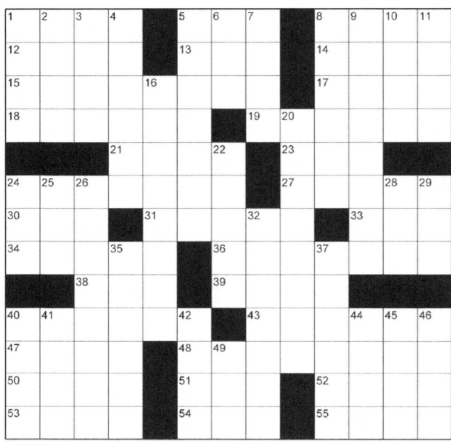

ACROSS
1. Parched
5. Chatter
8. Great quantity
12. 8th month of the Jewish calendar
13. In the past
14. Cab
15. Having many pages turned down so as to mark places (3-5)
17. Region
18. Small rocks
19. Parchment roll
21. Crustacean
23. Norse goddess
24. Temporary shelter in a battle zone
27. Decree
30. Highest mountain in Crete
31. Silly
33. Not
34. Tall and gangly
36. Erin
38. Brown shade
39. Pitch
40. Carry with great effort
43. Trapped
47. Freshwater duck
48. Precede in time
50. Singer
51. Sheltered side
52. Personalities
53. Valley
54. Prefix, foot
55. Humid

DOWN
1. Helps
2. Indian peasant
3. The villain in Othello
4. Soak
5. Sweet fortified wine of Sicily
6. Mature
7. Deities
8. Gaped
9. U.S. States, North and South -
10. Jump in figure skating
11. Face
16. Heavier-than-air craft
20. American Indian
22. Suit
24. An evergreen
25. Room within a harem
26. Salt of xanthic acid
28. Is able to
29. Spread out for drying
32. Covered with frost
35. Fluids measure
37. Containing tetraethyllead
40. Male deer
41. Prison room
42. Insect feeler
44. Hindu music
45. English college
46. Writing table
49. Born

Puzzle 82

ACROSS
1. Inspires dread
5. Government broadcaster
8. Heroic story
12. Take by force
13. Victory sign
14. Once again
15. Having a softer and smoother texture
17. Pit
18. Tilted over (Ship)
19. Rubbed out
21. A Great Lake
23. Anger
24. State of being acid
27. Of course
30. Prefix, over
31. Expiring
33. Also
34. Caravansary
36. Closest
38. Highest mountain in Crete
39. Deride
40. Carts
43. Valleys
47. Brown and white horse
48. Book of the Bible
50. Monetary unit of Peru
51. Dined
52. Gaelic
53. Golf mounds
54. Goad for driving cattle
55. Property title

DOWN
1. Curved entrance
2. Item of merchandise
3. Fencing sword
4. Closed tightly
5. Eagerness
6. Hive insect
7. Wax
8. Elm fruit
9. Aniseed liqueur
10. Hereditary factor
11. Overwhelmed
16. Of midday
20. Able to be rung
22. Watching
24. Donkey
25. Prompt
26. Supply with water
28. Long-leaved lettuce
29. Torrid
32. Whinnied
35. Handsome man
37. Bored out
40. Subpoena
41. First class (1-3)
42. Catch
44. Dreadful
45. Relax
46. Outbuilding
49. Greek letter

Puzzle 83

40. Determine
43. Peyote
47. Ireland
48. Distinction
50. Quote
51. Charged particle
52. Single items
53. Unlocking implements
54. Prefix, whale
55. Pause

DOWN
1. Root of the taro
2. Knights' titles
3. Weave wool
4. Shouted
5. Ancient galley
6. An age
7. Brink
8. Last syllable of a word
9. Containing mercury
10. Root vegetable
11. Food scraps
16. Made smooth
20. Announces formally
22. Music, sign
24. Intention
25. Dove's call
26. Daring
28. Poem
29. - Vegas, US gambling city
32. Supplement
35. Dresses which flare from the top (1-5)
37. Wise old man
40. Ship's floor
41. A Great Lake
42. Heroic
44. Motion picture
45. Matures
46. For fear that
49. Fish eggs

ACROSS
1. Portable ice-box
5. Golf peg
8. Boss on a shield
12. Eat
13. Metal bar
14. Ogle
15. Boring
17. Weight allowance
18. Stableman
19. Decrees
21. Days before

23. Australian bird
24. Academic community
27. Song
30. Acknowledgement of debt
31. Lawful
33. Highest mountain in Crete
34. Pertaining to mode
36. Shades of meaning
38. Beer
39. Monster

Puzzle 84

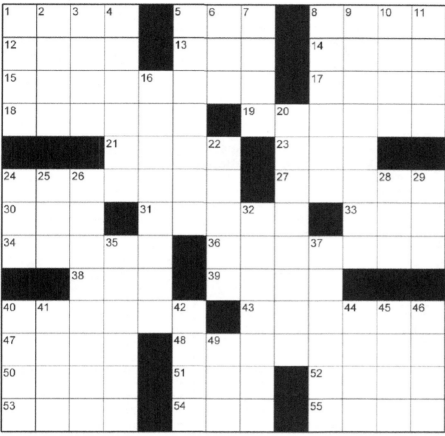

43. Footless
47. Jump
48. Pimenta dioica
50. Incite
51. Fish eggs
52. Prefix, eight
53. Minus
54. Abstract being
55. Writing table

DOWN
1. Summit of a small hill
2. Detest
3. Poker stake
4. Hammered in spikes
5. Bull-like
6. Brick carrier
7. Supplements
8. Remove by melting
9. Goes on
10. Ireland
11. Prophet
16. Resembling a monster
20. Root vegetables
22. Weird
24. Laboratory
25. Highest mountain in Crete
26. Fodder sacks hung from horses' heads
28. Owing
29. Distress signal
32. Confidences
35. Escarpments
37. Type of crustacean
40. 12th month of the Jewish calendar
41. Lake
42. Lively
44. Cube
45. Performs
46. Lose water
49. Actor, - Chaney

ACROSS
1. Persian lord
5. Definite article
8. Primates
12. Grandmother
13. Very good (1-2)
14. French cheese
15. Stance
17. Tradition
18. Vegetable skinner
19. Shim
21. A Great Lake

23. Dined
24. Insecticide and weed-killer
27. Marsh plants
30. Fuss
31. Expressions
33. Twosome
34. Bass singer
36. Changes into ions
38. Biblical high priest
39. Greek goddess of strife
40. To comprise

Puzzle 85

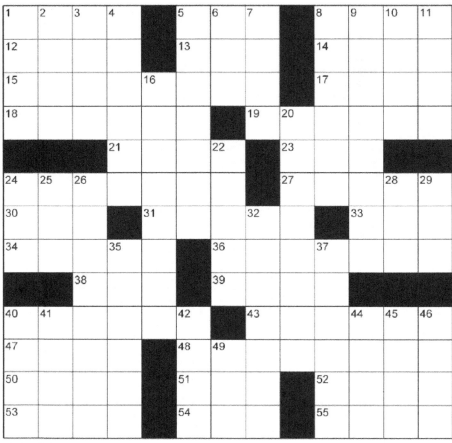

ACROSS
1. Blue-gray
5. An age
8. Sinister
12. Lubricates
13. Greek letter
14. Green stone
15. Part of a whole
17. Australian super-model
18. Wheel giving rides at show
19. Self-supporting structures
21. Food scraps
23. Greek letter

24. Unit of magnetic flux
27. Hood-shaped anatomical part
30. Wood sorrel
31. Monetary unit of Sierra Leone
33. Allow
34. The sesame plant
36. Shipping route (3.4)
38. It is
39. Fleet rodent
40. Shocked with horror

43. Get back
47. Smart - , show-off
48. Unfit to be eaten
50. Indian queen
51. Greek goddess of the dawn
52. Off-Broadway theater award
53. Paradise
54. Once common, now banned, insecticide
55. Close to

DOWN
1. A hit
2. Italian currency
3. Having wings
4. Trust deed
5. Letter
6. Exclamation of surprise
7. One of Columbus's ships
8. Matter erupted from a volcano
9. The hall of Odin
10. Lazy
11. Dregs
16. Unwearying
20. Changed ratios of cogs
22. Splash through mud
24. Unruly crowd
25. Top card
26. Yellow, crystalline fungicide
28. Even (poet.)
29. Dined
32. Closest
35. Nicotinic acid
37. Multitude
40. River in central Switzerland
41. Pleased
42. Bound
44. French clergyman
45. Hip bones
46. Never
49. Indicate assent

ANSWER KEY

Solution 1

Solution 2

Solution 3

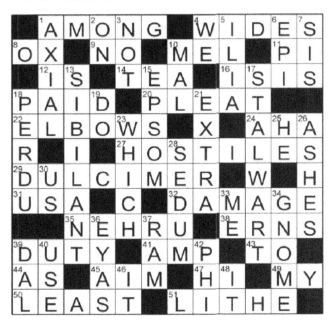

Solution 4

Solution 5

Solution 6

Solution 7

Solution 8

Solution 9

Solution 10

Solution 11

Solution 12

Solution 13

Solution 14

Solution 15

Solution 16

Solution 17

O	L	I	D		R	E	G	O		S	E	A
B	E	A	R		I	N	N	S		H	A	G
S	A	M	E		T	O	U	T		I	V	E
		A	N	E	W		L	O	V	E	R
S	P	A	D	E	S		V	E	X	
E	R	R	E	D		E	A	R		E	S	P
C	O	E	D		F	A	N		B	R	I	E
T	W	A		C	E	T		B	U	N	G	S
		B	A	Y		A	R	D	E	N	T
B	A	B	E	L		S	N	A	G	
O	C	A		A	G	O	G		E	N	V	Y
L	E	T		I	Y	A	R		T	O	E	A
E	R	E		S	P	R	Y		S	T	E	M

Solution 18

R	O	A	R		S	K	A	T		H	O	G
E	L	L	E		M	O	T	E		E	G	O
T	E	T	H		A	B	E	L		L	E	O
		E	U	R	O		L	U	M	E	N
T	A	L	E	N	T		M	E	S	
A	I	O	L	I		M	I	R		S	A	P
X	M	A	S		F	A	X		K	I	N	A
I	S	M		W	E	B		B	I	S	O	N
		B	A	D		F	A	D	I	N	G
E	B	B	E	D		K	L	A	N	
R	E	E		E	T	U	I		A	R	T	Y
G	A	D		R	I	D	E		P	O	R	E
O	D	E		S	L	U	R		S	M	I	T

Solution 19

B	U	S	Y		O	R	A	D		S	B	S
A	P	I	A		M	E	S	A		N	A	E
A	S	P	S		E	S	K	Y		O	L	E
		H	I	G	H		F	I	B	E	R
A	L	U	M	N	A		U	L	T	
B	A	L	A	S		B	E	Y		I	D	E
L	I	N	K		R	A	Y		B	O	R	A
E	R	A		O	O	H		M	U	T	E	S
		B	A	T		S	I	L	A	G	E
C	H	I	E	F		S	T	A	R	
O	U	T		I	N	K	Y		U	S	E	S
I	L	E		S	A	I	L		S	A	R	I
N	A	M		H	Y	P	E		H	O	R	N

Solution 20

B	R	A	W		R	A	N	K		E	F	T
A	E	R	O		E	D	E	N		W	E	E
D	E	E	M		E	D	G	E		E	E	N
		B	I	D	S		L	A	R	D	S
N	O	P	A	L	S		E	L	M	
A	B	A	T	E		G	A	S		T	A	M
O	O	P	S		F	U	R		P	I	K	E
S	E	A		J	A	M		T	I	K	I	S
		N	I	X		S	A	V	I	N	S
M	A	G	O	G		O	H	I	O	
U	G	H		G	A	V	E		T	O	T	S
T	E	E		E	P	E	E		A	B	E	T
E	R	E		R	E	N	T		L	I	N	Y

Solution 21

Solution 22

Solution 23

Solution 24

Solution 25

T	H	E		H	A	A	G			D	A	B
O	U	R		E	C	H	O		N	E	M	O
G	E	R	B	E	R	A		R	A	C	E	R
			I	D	E		B	E	Z	A	N	T
S	E	R	F	S		G	E	L	I	D		
L	I	E	F		S	A	N	E		E	G	O
A	R	E		S	W	U	N	G		N	A	P
B	E	N		A	I	D	E		S	C	O	T
		T	O	M	M	Y		G	A	E	L	S
K	E	R	N	O	S		P	L	Y			
A	B	A	C	A		P	E	A	S	A	N	T
N	O	N	E		D	E	E	D		Y	A	W
A	N	T		O	G	L	E			E	T	A

Solution 26

T	W	A		P	L	E	A			G	A	B
A	A	H		L	E	E	S		C	E	L	L
I	T	A	L	I	A	N		C	E	A	S	E
			O	C	H		H	A	R	R	O	W
A	M	E	B	A		B	E	D	E	W		
G	O	R	E		H	E	L	D		H	I	P
I	D	O		H	U	R	L	Y		E	T	A
N	E	G		E	R	G	O		P	E	E	L
		E	Y	E	R	S		B	A	L	M	S
L	O	N	E	L	Y		F	Y	N			
A	V	O	W	S		M	A	T	E	L	O	T
Z	E	U	S		S	A	K	E		O	N	E
E	N	S		O	D	E	S			G	O	A

Solution 27

R	O	B		R	E	G	O			F	B	I
O	N	E		I	Y	A	R		P	O	O	L
M	O	N	S	T	E	R		A	I	O	L	I
			T	E	D		R	U	S	T	L	E
T	U	B	A	S		F	E	R	A	L		
E	M	I	R		C	A	N	A		O	R	B
A	B	C		Y	O	D	E	L		O	H	O
T	O	O		A	N	E	W		U	S	E	R
		N	E	W	T	S		C	L	E	A	N
L	O	C	A	L	E		N	O	N			
A	M	A	S	S		R	E	W	A	R	D	S
C	A	V	E		D	I	M	E		A	U	K
E	R	E		O	D	O	R			G	O	A

Solution 28

M	E	N		I	B	I	S			G	Y	M
A	T	E		N	O	N	O		B	L	A	E
L	A	B	O	U	R	S		P	O	U	R	S
			B	R	A		R	E	W	E	D	S
M	A	R	I	E		F	I	T	L	Y		
A	B	E	T		C	A	V	E		N	E	D
A	B	C		B	A	K	E	R		E	A	U
M	A	E		E	R	I	N		P	S	S	T
		N	A	G	O	R		M	O	S	E	Y
G	O	S	P	E	L		D	I	E			
A	G	I	S	T		S	A	L	T	A	N	T
F	L	O	E		M	A	N	E		B	A	A
F	E	N		E	G	G	S			Y	E	T

Solution 29

Solution 30

Solution 31

Solution 32

Solution 33

W	O	E			H	E	F	T			N	O	V	A
A	R	E			E	Y	E	R			O	V	E	N
G	E	R	M	F	R	E	E			D	U	R	O	
			I	O	T	A			M	A	D	M	A	N
A	N	N	O	Y			O	B	E	Y				
W	E	E	D			S	I	L	O			B	O	D
E	M	S			G	A	L	E	N			U	N	I
S	O	S			O	N	E	S			G	L	U	E
				T	B	A	R			A	A	L	S	T
A	L	B	E	I	T			A	B	L	Y			
I	Y	A	R			I	N	V	I	A	B	L	E	
D	R	A	M			V	O	I	D			O	A	F
E	E	L	S			E	R	S	E			Y	E	T

Solution 34

G	A	R			S	T	A	B			T	A	B	S
O	B	I			M	A	N	E			A	L	O	E
D	Y	S	L	E	X	I	A			H	A	L	T	
			K	A	L	I			N	O	O	S	E	S
F	A	I	N	T			A	B	L	E				
L	E	E	K			D	E	A	L			V	A	S
E	R	S			T	E	S	L	A			O	I	L
D	O	T			S	T	O	L			R	I	D	E
				C	A	R	P			B	E	D	E	W
S	A	F	A	R	I			M	E	G	A			
A	L	A	R			T	R	I	G	O	N	A	L	
R	E	I	N			U	P	D	O			C	H	E
D	E	N	Y			S	M	I	T			E	A	T

Solution 35

L	A	X			A	P	E	D			M	A	T	S
O	N	E			S	E	R	E			O	B	I	E
W	I	N	D	W	A	R	D			U	L	N	A	
			O	R	A	L			I	S	L	E	T	S
J	A	P	A	N			S	C	O	T				
A	C	H	Y			C	O	A	L			E	O	S
W	H	O			P	H	O	T	O			T	W	O
S	E	N			L	A	K	E			D	E	E	D
				B	O	S	S			S	U	R	R	A
A	N	S	E	T	T			S	T	E	N			
F	A	N	G			I	D	E	A	L	I	T	Y	
A	P	I	A			T	I	L	L			T	O	E
R	A	P	T			Y	E	L	L			Y	O	N

Solution 36

M	U	D			I	M	A	M			C	Y	M	E
R	E	E			C	O	N	E			R	O	O	D
S	Y	M	B	O	L	I	C			O	L	I	D	
			E	R	N	E			H	A	C	K	L	Y
C	A	N	I	S			J	A	R	S				
R	O	T	E			P	E	N	T			F	A	R
U	N	I			T	H	A	I	S			I	D	O
S	E	A			S	Y	N	C			T	R	A	D
				P	A	L	S			P	O	E	M	S
A	W	H	I	R	L			A	R	I	D			
D	E	A	N			O	E	N	O	L	O	G	Y	
D	A	Z	E			I	N	N	S			G	O	A
S	L	E	D			D	D	A	Y			S	O	H

Solution 37

Solution 38

Solution 39

Solution 40

Solution 41

Solution 42

Solution 43

Solution 44

Solution 45

Solution 46

Solution 47

Solution 48

Solution 49

U	S	A			V	O	I	D			S	P	A
H	O	U	R		A	P	S	E		H	U	G	
F	U	R	Y		L	E	A	F	L	I	K	E	
		I	O	N	I	C		E	L	V	E	R	
W	A	F	T	E	D		E	R	A				
I	D	O		B	A	U	M		N	U	D	E	
D	A	R	E		T	E	E		O	N	E	R	
E	M	M	Y		E	Y	R	A		B	A	G	
		R	E	D		G	I	G	O	L	O		
C	O	B	I	A		H	E	R	O	D			
A	L	L	E	R	G	E	N		L	I	S	P	
P	I	E		L	A	I	C		D	E	A	R	
S	O	B		S	P	R	Y		D	O	E		

Solution 50

C	U	E		D	E	R	M		A	L	E
U	S	E	D		E	R	I	E		G	I	T
B	A	R	E		V	I	G	N	E	R	O	N
	I	B	S	E	N		D	I	A	N	A
G	U	N	S	E	L		L	S	D	
I	R	E		A	O	N	E		E	G	A	D
V	A	S	E		P	O	I		R	A	N	I
E	L	S	E		E	R	S	E		I	T	S
		R	A	D		U	R	A	N	I	C
P	L	A	I	D		E	R	N	E	S	
R	A	C	E	M	A	T	E		O	A	R	S
E	K	E		I	D	O	L		N	Y	E	T
Y	E	R		T	O	N	Y		S	P	Y

Solution 51

H	A	R	P		O	A	F		M	A	P	S
A	Y	A	H		R	H	O		E	L	S	E
Y	E	L	L		I	A	M		R	E	S	T
	S	E	E	D	S		E	D	I	C	T	
			G	E	O		N	O	N			
S	E	A	M	E	N		T	R	O	C	H	E
A	L	L						E	O	N		
Y	I	E	L	D	S		G	U	L	P	E	D
		U	E	Y		I	S	A				
B	O	M	B	S		B	A	N	T	U		
B	A	R	B		T	A	B		C	O	P	E
O	R	C	A		E	R	E		E	G	O	S
G	N	A	R		M	E	T		R	A	N	T

Solution 52

E	R	S	E		J	A	R		B	A	L	I
F	A	T	S		O	C	A		E	G	A	D
T	I	E	S		Y	E	S		T	I	D	E
D	W	A	R	F		C	O	I	N	S		
		Y	O	U		A	D	D			
W	E	A	S	E	L		L	E	E	R	E	D
E	R	N							A	T	E	
D	R	I	V	E	N		T	R	O	J	A	N
	U	N	I		O	H	O				
D	U	L	S	E		I	O	D	I	C	
S	Y	N	C		C	O	L		L	O	O	M
I	N	C	A		E	R	E		E	T	N	A
N	E	O	N		S	E	T		S	A	K	E

Solution 53

Solution 54

Solution 55

Solution 56

Solution 57

Solution 58

Solution 59

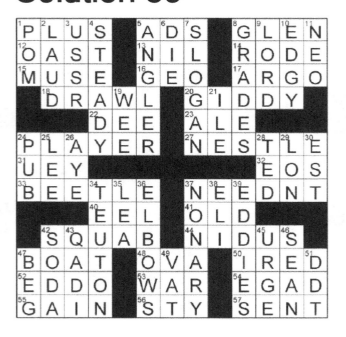

Solution 60

Solution 61

Solution 62

Solution 63

Solution 64

Solution 65

D	O	L	E		F	A	D		B	L	E	W
O	V	E	R		R	H	O		L	O	R	E
S	I	V	A		A	A	H		O	B	I	T
E	D	I	S	O	N			I	C	O	N	S
			U	P	C	A	S	T				
G	E	N	R	E		T	I	S		B	E	N
A	L	O	E		M	I	X		T	A	L	A
G	I	N		B	E	L		E	E	R	I	E
			O	T	T	A	W	A				
K	O	T	O	W		D	E	C	A	D	E	
U	P	O	N		I	D	A		H	A	U	L
D	A	L	E		L	A	G		E	R	A	S
O	L	D	S		L	Y	E		R	E	D	E

Solution 66

B	L	O	W		S	I	S		T	A	P	E
R	O	P	E		M	O	A		A	G	E	R
E	V	E	S		I	N	N		X	I	A	N
N	E	C	T	A	R			P	I	N	T	S
			E	S	K	I	E	S				
S	O	A	R	S		T	R	I		G	I	G
P	A	I	N		W	A	S		D	A	T	E
A	R	M		D	A	L		P	O	S	S	E
			A	N	Y	H	O	W				
P	L	U	M	B			A	D	A	G	E	S
Y	A	R	E		J	A	M		G	O	T	H
R	I	T	E		O	V	A		E	R	N	E
E	D	I	T		B	E	L		R	E	A	M

Solution 67

R	I	F	T		M	U	M		M	O	D	E
A	R	E	A		I	S	A		E	P	E	E
T	I	E	R		D	A	B		M	A	L	L
E	S	D	R	A	S			L	O	L	L	S
			I	N	T	O	T	O				
P	A	G	E	D		R	O	B		I	O	N
A	P	E	D		B	A	R		A	N	N	A
D	E	E		A	R	C		O	N	S	E	T
			M	A	H	O	U	T				
B	U	T	S	U			A	D	A	G	E	S
A	R	I	A		M	E	R		C	U	B	A
N	A	R	K		O	R	E		I	R	O	N
E	L	L	E		B	A	D		D	U	N	K

Solution 68

S	E	L	L		L	U	G		M	O	L	E
A	L	E	E		I	S	A		A	V	O	N
N	A	T	O		B	A	R		I	A	G	O
K	N	O	T	T	Y			A	L	L	O	W
			A	N	A	D	E	M				
C	H	E	R	T		A	M	P		E	R	E
H	A	N	D		A	D	S		S	L	U	R
E	O	S		R	A	D		I	C	I	E	R
			P	H	Y	L	L	O				
L	O	C	U	M			E	L	F	I	S	H
O	A	R	S		G	U	V		F	L	E	A
G	H	E	E		A	N	I		E	K	E	S
S	U	E	D		S	I	S		D	A	M	P

Solution 69

Solution 70

Solution 71

Solution 72

Solution 73

Solution 74

Solution 75

Solution 76

Solution 77

Solution 78

Solution 79

Solution 80

Solution 81

Solution 82

Solution 83

Solution 84

Solution 85

B	L	A	E		E	O	N		E	V	I	L
O	I	L	S		P	H	I		J	A	D	E
F	R	A	C	T	I	O	N		E	L	L	E
F	E	R	R	I	S		A	R	C	H	E	S
			O	R	T	S		E	T	A		
M	A	X	W	E	L	L		G	A	L	E	A
O	C	A		L	E	O	N	E		L	E	T
B	E	N	N	E		S	E	A	L	A	N	E
		T	I	S		H	A	R	E			
A	G	H	A	S	T		R	E	G	A	I	N
A	L	E	C		I	N	E	D	I	B	L	E
R	A	N	I		E	O	S		O	B	I	E
E	D	E	N		D	D	T		N	E	A	R

Made in the USA
Monee, IL
09 February 2023

27370140R00063